Walking Alone Together

An Anthem to Care Givers

by

Marina Brown,
R.N., B.S.N., M.S.N. Ed.

A hospice nurse presents a collection of beautiful lives with workbook pages for you to include your own loved one within their ranks

Contents

FOREWARD

It seems that by definition, paths are not straight.

Sidewalks are straight. Highways stretch for miles without a curve—but paths are bumpy and twisting, littered with obstacles. They slow us down, make us pay attention, test our strength, but in the end, are often the most beautiful way to have followed.

My patients had all traveled other routes before their lives took the turn that led them onto their final paths. Some had been dynamos with high-powered jobs; some from countries most Americans only vaguely know. Some of my patients were gentle, and some were feisty curmudgeons who lived out their final illnesses with the same bombast they'd lived their lives. But whether with family beside them or not, they made their journey alone, stepping onto the solitary path and into a future that is, in fact, an end. And yet, I have not seen one person do it without courage and heroism. Nor have the people who took care of those preparing to leave.

Often in the last week or so of a person's life, I had the impression that while both of my patients' feet had previously been on land with a little boat nearby, very subtly, their weight had shifted, one foot now in the skiff. Eventually, the second foot came aboard, and without fanfare, without our really knowing, they had left—even before their body was gone.

It was in this period, when my patients had relinquished ties with this world, that I found them to be in what one might call a 'state of grace'—detached, at peace, gaze fixed elsewhere and away. It was for those left behind that confusion sometimes remained—the way worried parents feel when they see their child happily turning to run and join their new friends at summer camp.

It is especially to those who, for now, are staying on the shore that this book is intended. And to those who have truly and finally gone that honor is given.

The path that the terminally-ill patient follows is one that only he or she can walk, it is his own and unique—and he must ultimately finish the journey alone. And yet, as long as there are humans amongst us, we walk with them; we watch them; we learn from them how to do it.

And so I offer these stories of very brave people to very brave people—those who will walk together down the path that the loved one takes alone.

It has been a privilege for me to sometimes join them.

HONORARIA

Yesterday John died. I had McDonald's
                              with extra fries.

Walter died today. I bought matching lampshades
                                    for the den.

Albert died in the hospital. I helped my daughter
                              study for her science test.

Kathy died yesterday—she was 31. My Christmas
                              shopping is almost done.

Anne died overnight. I've put geraniums all around
                                    the patio.

Gregory died in the arms of his sister. I picked up
                              Greek food for dinner.

And Kathy and Anne, Albert and Greg,
Walter and thoughtful John
Vibrant and real and forever alive inside of me,

Because you no longer can,
I laugh in the sun and I sing in the winter,

And I do these things for each of you.

Marina Brown

A Love Song

By day the swirling paisley and embroidered silk layered the bed, a rich and confused chaos of fabric that engulfed the slim outline within. But at twilight, in the soft blue haze that seemed to seep through the curtains, I could see more clearly the outline as it rose and fell, hovered in silence, then, with a rustle, readjusted and rose and fell again.

I knew that she preferred this time of day, when the noises of the living became preoccupied and quiet, and even the birds turned away. I knew that in the twilight, her eyes, white and wide open, would wander the shadows finding texture and form.

The figure beneath the fabric stirred, and her head turned slowly as if a melody had begun. I knew that she was remembering.

*

Meilong's black hair lies damp along her neck. The steamy Vietnamese road is splashed with shadows. She is full of youth and doesn't want the dust of the path on her dress. It is white and clean, and she is filled with spring and the sound of a war gone silent.

Ahead she sees the old women and slows as she watches them stoop to gather stones from the road. Like gulls, the old women chatter and dart forward and back, each with a stone and a curse aimed for the clean white dress, at this girl who speaks Vietnamese but is an alien among them.

Born from a black soldier and a local girl's shame and left to toddle alone in the streets of Saigon, Meilong was one day swept up by an elderly teacher and taken home to his wife to raise.

Mississippi-chocolate skin, wild black hair flying in little helixes around the high cheekbones and tilted eyes of Asia, her face told too well of a night that her countrymen would not let her forget—a face an old man found perfect and beautiful.

*

She coughed in the deepening dusk and from beneath the quilt, a frail arm extended toward a tiny radio and, with effort, switched it on. The crackling of a faraway station drifted fragments of Vietnamese music about her bed.

She curled close to the tiny machine, her head, bald, with tiny sores dotting her skin. She began to hum and the bones of her fingers were moving. She was remembering again.

*

The refugee camp in Thailand is bleak; tents or tin and paper shacks stretch for acres. Meilong and her elderly parents have lived here for four years. People come and go, but doctors doctor and teachers teach, and slowly a community has evolved.

It is at the camp, in a tin corrugated building to which Meilong goes each day, that she has learned the ancient instrument of Vietnam. The *thu cam*, a tall, stringed, harp-like device, is filled with the throb of longing hearts. As Meilong plays and sings, her graying teachers, who know they will never return home, nod at this half-Asian, half-black girl, and tell her that the soul of Saigon is in her voice and in her hands.

But others hate her for it. One night as she sings for herself on a little rise overlooking the camp, sheltered with her harp in a thin stand of bamboo—she is raped. Cruelly and with the anger of the giftless for the gifted, she is raped, and her fingers are broken. With the fury of one color for another unlike itself, she is beaten. Just as cruelly, they leave the *thu cam* untouched beside her, never to sing her song again.

*

In the quiet American town, the tiny man kneels before her. He is old, with a permanent smile and blinking eyes which seem perpetually wishing to understand. He places his hand on her shoulder and offers her tea. In the near darkness I see her turn. Her eyes, white as moons, never leave his face.

If he wants to understand, she is willing him to know—and yet, she cannot tell him.

A passionate bond unites the old teacher and his once beautiful, half-black child. For her, the one remaining dream has been of this devoted father, to live long enough to care for him in his old age, as a child should do for her parent.

She feels humiliated by this illness and hates its shame. Yet it is the shame of others that she wears on her face and carries in her body, shame she has chosen to endure with grace.

With a Chinese herb, her father rubs her fingers, which often ache. The fingers are twisted and tight, but every night he tries to stretch them. Her eyes never leave his face. I once asked her if her father knew about the AIDS, and how she had been infected, and she told me that one day she would tell him, but she believed on that day he would stop loving her.

Meilong's pain grew worse. She rarely slept and moaned softly when she did. The old man asked me the name of this illness that had entrapped his daughter, yet with discretion, I could not tell him.

But Meilong had heard his questions and whispered that, at last, the time had come. That evening, I watched from afar as she pulled herself up and into a kneeling posture before her father. I had never seen her so thin, so weak. Her body trembled beneath the gauze pajamas. Silhouetted in the dusk, he seemed a Buddha, distant and unknowable, she a penitent for whom redemption was impossible and only honor remained.

Slowly she bowed her head three times to the floor, and the old man leaned closer. Her voice came as a murmur, guttural, rhythmic, halting. She spoke until her strength had fled and the words were all used up.

When she was finished, the old man rose. He looked out at the trees, black, with the brittle chrome outline of the new moon. Then without a word or a touch he walked silently from the room. Meilong did not move. Finally she pulled her arms about her head and wept.

A week passed. Meilong had drawn near death. Her breathing was rapid and she was conscious only from time to time. The old man stayed away. The tea had stopped and he no longer stroked her fingers. It seemed that she had been right; his love had been withdrawn, the shame too much even for this affectionate old man.

And then on the day before she died, the door to the house quietly opened. Softly, musicians removed their shoes and filed silently into the room. They bowed to the elder father, then to Meilong, around whose tiny wrists they tied white prayer threads. Without speaking a word, they arranged themselves around her pallet and began to play.

The old man sat alone on a chair, eyes fixed on the ceiling. Plucked and bowed instruments, soft drums, jingling cymbals, the musicians chanted in the voice of a faraway land.

Meilong's eyes opened. She might have believed herself in paradise. The fragile muscles of her face pulled into a smile, and she gazed from one instrument to the next. These were her songs singing to her again. This was her father's gift—his gift of love, not withdrawn, but compounded.

Meilong reached weakly for her father's hand. Her eyes were hollow but riveted upon his face. Without looking at her, as the tears cursed down his wrinkled cheeks, the old man's hand stretched down to hers, and he held her little fingers. Slowly, he stroked them—gently, ever so gently, he stroked her little fingers.

A Love Song: Each of us holds something of which we are ashamed and for which we feel there may be no forgiveness. Is there something for which your loved one or you needs to ask if forgiveness could be given?

_____

_____

_____

_____

_____

_____

_____

_____

_____

_____

_____

_____

_____

_____

_____

_____

THE FLOWER BOX

I was preparing to leave when I heard the faint clatter of Randolph's cart. It was a noise that always accompanied the old man when he approached—at least in the early days. Sometimes the rattles were drowned out by the other sounds—the white roar of the highway traffic, the occasional shriek of brakes, or the frustration of horns as commuters jockeyed for position on the over-pass above.

Randolph lived beneath the cacophony—in a small world where he needed little. There was his shopping cart, which he called his 'vehicular transportation"; his box, a semi-solid refrigerator carton into which he would crawl each night; and a symbol of luxury, a permanently damp, pinkish blanket under which each night he would fall into the deep sleep of proud homeowners everywhere.

Randolph's box was between the cardboard enclosures of Zack and Charles, two of his neighbors in this formerly dangerous amalgam of men consigned to life in the rough. But with the aesthetic of a good homeowner's association, they had all positioned empty tin cans in neat rows in front of their boxes to form a hobo's version of a white-picket fence.

If life success was about having staked out a tiny patch of one's own terra firma, Randolph, Charles and Zack were all achievers.

Randolph was rattling closer now, shoving the grocery cart piled high with clothes, an extra pair of sneakers, a bent-eared calendar, a discreetly covered roll of toilet paper, and a large black trash bag stuffed with what Randolph considered the contents of his 'desk'. Over it all he positioned his pink blanket, topping it off with a weathered poncho. He also, incongruously, carried a garden trowel that he was never without.

It was the first time I had seen him in two weeks. Randolph was frequently 'not home' under the overpass. But if I were lucky, I might find him asleep beside a downtown fountain in the park, or tucked in the doorway of the Social Security office where he claimed he'd been so many times that a stop-off there was like visiting friends.

But today, something was different. I could see it in the form his dark silhouette made as he pushed his cart over a curb toward his box. This time I couldn't see his head over the jostling mound of debris that formed his life.

I was worried. For hard as it was, holding his head up high was something Randolph had always managed to do.

That head and all that went with it was the first challenge that Randolph had faced, and his body and its twisted limbs seemed but the rehearsal for all the other adversity that followed.

Randolph had been abandoned 68 years ago in a trash can near a church in downtown St. Louis. The orphanage that took over his care quickly discovered that several miracles would be needed if the permanently squalling black baby boy were to survive. His bald head was too big; his tiny back disfigured; his tongue protruded; and at the end of a shriveled left leg was a clubbed foot that seemed only good for kicking. One nun used to tell him his leathery skin gave him a reptilian look. Certainly, this infant was not one that would be adopted. The sight of baby Randolph didn't command love.

But somehow he earned it. He survived his first year, and then his second. Randolph didn't walk for another two. And when he did, his curved spine and clubbed foot gave him the look of a scurrying crab, with long arms reaching out for things to hold on to and a large head tilted like a crustacean's for a better view. But as time went on, most days would find Randolph scrambling with a purpose—heading for the garden behind the orphanage, the place where he thought he'd found heaven.

Old men like the orphanage groundskeeper, Mr. Puckett, are often about as lonely as—little black boys whose heads overshadow their shoulders or whose voices resemble growling crickets. And so it was fitting that amidst the rows of gladiolas and mums and lilacs and roses that Mr. Puckett had planted in a burst of horticultural creativity, that the old man and the little twisted boy found each other. With his nose buried in the blossom of a yellow rose or on his knees pulling weeds from around the glads, nobody could tell Randolph from any other little boy. And Mr. Puckett loved him. The old gardener liked nothing better than to see the joy in his little acolyte's face when, every Friday, he would reward Randolph with a fragrant bouquet to carry back to the dormitory's beige bleakness—and a squeeze around Randolph's shoulders that made the boy giggle and nuzzle the old man back.

As time went on, they enlarged the garden. With seed catalogs laid out before them, they sketched spots for vegetables and ground fruits. They put in a few flowering trees. When he was eleven, Randolph even presented Mr. Puckett with a drawing of a pond and a little arched bridge that would be surrounded with bowers of jasmine and pink bouganvilla—and maybe even a little gazebo where Mr. Puckett, who was having a harder and harder time walking, could sit and watch the colors of the garden turn as the season changed. Those were the times that Randolph almost forgot that he still reminded people of an awkward crab or that his head was too big or that his skin was as bumpy as a lizard's.

He'd almost forgotten until the day Mr. Puckett died. And on that day, Randolph's real life resumed, and the idyll in the garden disappeared forever.

In those days, orphanages tried to support themselves. When children turned twelve most of them were pressed into real work for the community or as they grew older, turned out as near-slaves to locals who knew a good thing when they saw it. Randolph was a hard worker, the orphanage's sisters knew that. But most of the jobs as domestics or cleaning personnel needed to be filled by orphans who were— presentable. Randolph fit no bill that could make the facility money, and so he began a life below the orphanage, stoking the steam furnaces with coal, cleaning out weeping pipes and sorting through the garbage. These were jobs that would last until in his twenties, someone remembered the black 'gargoyle', as he was now dubbed, and that it was time for him to go.

The only things Randolph took with him the day he was turned out were a cardboard suitcase, a trowel Mr. Puckett had given him, and cuttings from some of his favorite plants from the garden that had long since run to weeds with dreams scattered everywhere.

The years after that varied little. With no home or education, Randolph settled into the rut of those without resources or love. The little gargoyle became an easy target. He couldn't fight back when he was beaten. He couldn't resist when a larger man would take his few possessions. He became a fixture from the street at shelters and cold weather repositories for the down and out and as always, an object of derision by people only a rung or two higher on the downward ladder of despair. And yet Randolph's sweetness seemed untouched.

One afternoon as he shivered slightly under his blanket, Randolph told me a story that explained everything. Walking along a street, he had come upon a little old lady trying to rake the leaves from her front lawn. Randolph smiled a toothless grin as he described the chance encounter and pulled the pink blanket tighter around his shoulders.

"I be just push'in my cart along when this nice ole white lady, she just sat down on her front step and looked up at me like she know'd me her whole life. 'I be tired', she say to me. And I say to her, 'Well, don't mind if I hep you out do ya, M'am?' An she just poked this ole rake out at me and she say, 'Have a go at it, son,'." Randolph laughed his crackly laugh. "This ole white lady, she called me 'son'." And after that Randolph and the old lady became friends.

Though he never wanted to stray far from his box, soon Randolph became a fixture in the aging downtown neighborhood populated by elderly women and declining men. His 'white Mama' introduced him to her friends and soon Randolph was limping to the grocery for them, painting their fences, cutting their shrubs, and gratefully accepting their gifts of a sandwich or lemonade beneath the big magnolias or oaks discreetly far from the house. There had been a trace of the happiness he'd known with Mr. Puckett— working with his hands, often working in the soil. But if Randolph had had any illusions about the relationships with these elderly Southern folk, it was made clear to him one afternoon as he struggled behind his 'white MaMa', carrying a large potted plant for her veranda.

It had come from across the street in the sweet high-pitched drawl of another old lady, a woman who only the week before had given Randolph a fancy hand-me-down shirt, a gift he had treasured. "Well what you got the little monkey doin' today, Inez?", called out the woman from across the street. "I declare if he don't look like Toby the Chimp from the circus last year," she'd laughed.

And then shockingly, his 'Mama' had called back, "He may look like a chimp, but he ain't so smart." Both women had had a good laugh. And Randolph knew that his time with the white folks was at an end. He'd put the potted plant down in the middle of the sidewalk, and turned and walked back to his box, ignoring the angry calls that were now coming from both his 'MaMa' and her friend.

But he had his trowel and those two strong hands on powerful arms. And he decided to make his own world—one that would be beautiful and never hurt. For the next year, Randolph lugged dirt—stolen dirt, maybe—from parks and vacant lots. At night he claimed bedding plants of various colors and made cuttings from trees and flowering arbors that sprouted in a dozen glass jars near his box. Slowly, as spring came, the tiny hobo village beneath the highway began to burst with curving beds of blooms. A half empty bag of rye grass had turned into a lush green carpet. Petunias, impatiens, marigolds, and sunny daisies spilled over one another. At night, Randolph and his neighbors, Zack and Charles, and the other residents of this cardboard town would sit facing the lawn illuminated with the pink glow of halogen, talking about themselves, their old dreams, and their new project—the vegetable garden that they all planned to share.

By the time they'd dug in the pumpkins and squash and had the rows laid out, Fall was in the air. It was then that Randolph had gotten the news. The strange aching in his side hadn't been from clearing refuse from the plot where their vegetable garden would grow. It was a cancer that was quickly invading his pancreas.

Randolph never wanted to go to the hospital. He'd been forced to for a few tests, but after that he would invite me to join him at the fountain in the park, or as time went on, to sit beside his box, facing the expansive garden that was now aflame in chrysanthemums and late roses. He worried what would happen to all his work when he was gone—his neighbors had promised to keep the weeds out and bring water for sprinkling. Randolph had his doubts. He'd always worried what the police would do if there were ever trouble beneath the highway. But since the garden had come to dominate their lives, there never seemed time for petty squabbling. Now he hoped it was all safe in the hands of Zack and Charles.

During his last week, I visited Randolph many times a day. Pancreatic pain has a way of blurring all other senses and because he was living in the open, a nurse needed to administer his medicine almost constantly. He had accepted a pillow and a warm white blanket, but Randolph only wanted beneath him the thin pallet of cardboard that he'd slept on since he was young. And, of course, his flowers.

Zack and Charles kept a kind of vigil. Each time they took a new turn sitting near Randolph's feet, they would bring in another little floral offering, and each time Randolph would try to rouse to admire the new blossom and tighten his gnarled old hand around his friend's.

Slowly, the garden moved. From outside to in, chrysanthemums and peonies, roses, and a few straggling daisies, the men of the village plucked their garden to give to their friend. And that was the way Randolph died, the refrigerator carton acting as both bed and bower, casket and mausoleum. And the garden trowel placed upon his chest as a make-do cross.

They had had nothing, these men. Mistrusted and flung from society, they'd beaten each other with self-loathing and given up on the thinnest of their dreams—until the little black gargoyle had dreamed one for them—one filled with fragrance and grace.

The Flower Box: Randolph was unnoticed through much of his life. What about your loved one has gone unnoticed and unappreciated? How can you rectify it?

_____

_____

_____

_____

_____

_____

_____

_____

_____

_____

_____

_____

_____

_____

_____

THE LONG WAIT

Day Six: I guess I can admit it to you, Dear Diary, but I'd actually thought that after we stopped the feeding tube and giving Mother water, that the final moment would come soon...a matter of days. But it's been six. I mean, after so many years just lying in bed, not talking, not moving, nothing...I just had thought that food was the only thing that kept her going. I don't mind...it's really like a miracle. It means I'll have her with me a few more days.

I pinned her hair up and put a little make-up on her cheeks. I know she'd like that.

Day Eight: The nurse had said it wouldn't be long...not over a week. I guess the human body has just so much...moisture...in it. I understand that eventually, like in the desert, a person just becomes too dehydrated to go on. At least Mother looks comfortable…like she always has.

I couldn't help myself...I bought her a new nightie It's blue and she looks beautiful.

Day Ten: Even the nurse says this is unusual for a patient with Alzheimer's. I mean, no food or water in ten days. I thought ten days was the maximum a person could go without water. Food, okay...but no water? Mother looks even more tranquil than she used to when I was feeding her every day. I'm really tired.

*

Bill was tired. Tired of so much. A part of him wished the tiredness could go on forever, continuing to care for his mother the way he had done the last five years, the two of them a perfect duo of understanding, the perfect giver coupled with the perfect receptor of love. Yet another part of Bill knew that each 24-hour day was extracting too much: each day bathing his mother, each day carrying her to her commode, and later, learning to use what he called her 'paper panties', because he thought any other words wouldn't suit the elegant woman who'd always been his best friend. He wondered if he could continue. Then he wondered if he should 'go' first. Perhaps he should arrange it that they 'go' together. Many thoughts crossed Bill's mind. He was very tired.

But he was an intrepid caregiver. He'd learned to prepare feedings and manage the pumps; to change the bed with her still in it, singing to his mother as he rolled her back and forth, imagining she was humming along to the show tunes they'd both loved. He would arrange her hair, fussing over each curl the way a hairdresser might, and sketch his customer's interior designs in the chair next to her bed— holding up the finished product for the imagined smile of approval from the woman who was his mentor and never-flagging cheer-leader—hoping for a smile that had long since failed to appear.

Bill was tired, precariously balanced in the disorienting world between those who live and those who simply breathe. It was only his desire for what he had known and loved his whole life to continue that kept him repeating his rituals of filial love, and for years that had been enough.

But in the months before hospice, the tranquility of their routine had begun to fray. No matter how many times Bill adjusted his mother's position with silk bolsters and pillow supports, added a new mattress, redoubled his efforts at creams and soothing lotions, her thin skin had begun to break into areas of redness. He had used massage. When an area had broken down completely, he used warm lamps. He religiously turned and propped her against pressure on anyone of the multiple areas of failed skin so that he was spending most of his day watching a timer for the minute of the next major adjustment. And then the problems with the feeding tube began.

Both Bill and his mother were fastidious and formal. When she had been able to at least open her mouth and swallow, Bill had prepared elaborate trays, a rose or orchid blossom perched on each one. Although it would take an hour for her to finish a few bites of soft food, it would always seem like a proper dinner or lunch, a time when Bill would happily chat about new trends in furnishings or fabrics and regale her with hilarious anecdotes about his decorating clients. The arrival of the feeding tube had changed things somewhat, but Bill still took his lunches beside his mother, even as the pump slowly fed her drip by drip. And the years had passed.

And then her body began rejecting the infused feedings. Bill was frantic. While his mother seemed as serene and impassive as ever, breathing lightly and quietly, like Beauty adrift in a golden dream, the feedings simply would not go in. Tubing was flushed and changed and Bill lobbied for a new surgical procedure to set things right again. But the doctors agreed that the time for bold measures had passed—had perhaps had never really been there. Alzheimer's never triumphs dramatically, but only as the insidious pasting together of threads of memory, and paradoxically, unraveling the fabric of a life. And thus, the doctors had said, there was nothing to be done. Her time had come. It would be kinder to simply remove the tubes and allow the gentle old lady pass with peace.

And so Bill had begun a kind of solitary death watch, a vigil where grief was silenced only when he was changing his mother's bed, combing her hair, or rubbing lotion softly along her hands. Always alone, Bill had never married, had few friends outside of his professional life, and once, late at night, had admitted that he had given up hopes of ever being in love. "My mother always hoped I would find someone, but I don't think that was in the cards for me," he'd said.

*

Day Twelve: Dear Diary, People are coming now to help me with Mother. She hasn't changed. It's been so long without anything going into her body. I think she's thinner...I know she is. But she never complains, not even a little moan when she's turned. I wonder how she can hold out so long. I wonder why.

Larry painted her nails this morning. What a sweet thing to do. Larry is the new nurse...what a nice thing to do.

Day Thirteen: It feels a little like spring today. I opened the windows in Mother's room so she could hear the birds. A couple of rose-colored tulips have begun to bud...and I put lipstick on her the color of the flowers. Thirteen days. Thirteen days without food or water. One of the nurses said she'd never seen anything like it. She told me I should tell mother it is alright to go. I'll have to think about that.

Larry's mother died last year. We had a good talk. It's funny, like me, Larry has never found anyone. He invited me out for coffee.

*

On the fourteenth day since the feeding tube had been disconnected, I entered the room where, in the early twilight, Bill was sitting beside his mother's bed. I could hear her soft, even breathing. And I sensed someone else in the room. Bill looked up and smiled. "I asked Larry to stay if he could. I know it's his day off, but he doesn't mind, do you?" Bill looked over at the nurse sitting in a corner, who was smiling back.

"I had the talk with mother," Bill said. "It's amazing, I never thought I would be able to say those things. I know she'll understand it isn't about losing her, God knows I don't want that. But I told her how beautiful I know things will be once she's out of this body that's not working anymore. It's just time to change locations...like redecorating," he smiled sadly. "I only wonder, honestly, how it will happen," he said, looking up at me.

I was honest. I walked near to his mother and put my hand on her forehead, stroking it gently. It was cool and dry. "Bill, at some point your mother's breathing will change. She will have moments where she doesn't breathe at all, like holding her breath. Then it will resume. And then stop for long seconds again". And at that moment, I realized that something had happened. His mother had stopped breathing. I looked down at her. She seemed to be holding her breath. And then she took a deep inhalation, breathed a few times, only to stop again. I cleared my throat and continued, still with my hand smoothing her hair.

"Eventually, usually in the hours or days before death comes, there will be a period of restlessness or agitation. Some people seem to want to take off their clothing, others speak of wanting to 'go home' or get out of bed. It seems to be like being born, there is a period of work, of labor as the body this time begins the process of true dying." And beneath my hand, I could feel Bill's mother starting to move. Immobile for weeks, she suddenly was turning her head slowly from side to side, picking at the blanket with stiffened fingers and moving her legs. Bill stood up and Larry came beside him. I removed my hand.

"What is happening," asked Bill.

"I don't know," I replied. And then, "Do you want me to go on?" Bill sighed and came beside his mother, knelt down and whispered something in her ear. Then holding her hand, he said, "Go on."

Again I placed my hand on her head and said, "After some time, the restlessness changes, but her breathing may get faster. She may appear to be fighting for breath, but eventually it will begin to slow." At that moment, Bill's mother, who had been twisting beneath the covers, seemed to relax. No longer moving, her breathing began to come in slow heaves. "And finally," I said, barely believing what I was seeing, "The breathing will simply stop. You may have the feeling that her spirit has passed...or as if someone has left the room." And at that moment, Bill's mother took a long, full breath, and then, quite as peacefully, she didn't do it again.

The three of us stood around the bed, staring at the woman who, despite her astounding longevity in the face of negative intake, but who only minutes before had shown no signs of imminent death, was now gone. We each began sorting out a mixture of sadness, shock, relief, and on my part, disbelief, at what had just happened. And then Bill, came over, took my arm and led me to a far corner of the room. He was smiling. "You look surprised," he almost giggled. I was surprised—but now at Bill's demeanor. "I'm not surprised," he said. "I understand it all now. Mother was a wise old thing."

We sat down on the chintz-covered chairs where long ago he and his mother had had tea every morning. "Last night, I'd had the talk with Mother. I told her it was alright to go and that I'd be fine...and I think that set the stage," he said. "But I hadn't told her everything." He looked across the room where in the light beside his mother's bed, Larry was beginning to assemble a towel and sweet smelling soap.

"When I knelt down, I whispered something to her, something that I know she'd been waiting all this time to hear...something I could have never told her before. I told her I think I'd met someone I would come to love. "He squeezed my hand and smiled again. Then he joined Larry as together they ministered the last acts of kindness to an old woman, who if her son were right, was willing to wait and wait and wait until the torch of love could be passed.

The Long Wait: Devotion and patience. Are you willing to wait for the slow unfolding of the future, trusting in its outcome, yet savoring the present just as it is? How do you support your loved one in this effort?

_____

_____

_____

_____

_____

_____

_____

_____

_____

_____

_____

_____

_____

_____

_____

_____

PUT ON A HAPPY FACE

"Oh, what a beautiful morning...Oh what a beautiful day...". I heard Margret before I saw her. But the lilt in her little song made me wonder if I were preparing to knock on the wrong door. After all, inside waiting for me, was Charlie, her husband, whose prostate cancer had reached its final stages.

"Well hello!" came a dancing voice from behind some bushes. Margaret swung from around the corner of the house, a pair of shears in one hand and a clutch of spring flowers in the other. A straw hat and bright scarf around her neck suggested a photo cut from a ladies' magazine—something about how to garden without raising a sweat.

"I'm so glad you could come!" Margaret smiled, pulling off her gardening gloves. "I picked these just for you for our first meeting!" Putting her arm around my waist, she opened the door and ushered me into the sprawling foyer of their estate. "But let's chat over some iced tea, shall we?"

Margaret, in her sixties, was still dazzling. Her hair was spun in golden swirls, her figure athletic and tanned, and on her hands thousands of dollars in diamonds sparkled violently. Yet, as she poured the tea into cut-glass tumblers, I wasn't sure she knew who I was. Did I look like an emissary from a board on which she served? A museum docent? Perhaps somebody from the Junior League. But then, as brightly as if tossing a ringlet from her face, she included, "Oh, later, you'll probably want to see Charlie."

I did. And I knew he would not welcome it. Charles' cancer was deep in the bones of his pelvis and legs now. After extensive radiation to interrupt its spread, not only was he unable to walk, but the skin had deteriorated and now there was widespread infection. One of my jobs would be to remove the infected tissue—debridement—and apply healing, but painful medication.

"So how is your summer going?" she effervesced from a silk-covered chair beside me. "I know we may have to depart a little later than we'd expected, but Charlie and I are planning on Santorini for a week then visiting some friends in Rome right after. I think he'll be up and around by then, don't you?"

I looked at Margaret for a moment, searching for a hint of irony. Perhaps the doctors had spared her details of his illness. I guessed she knew I was a nurse, but that I would be Charlie's last nurse, she didn't seem to grasp.

I leaned closer, hoping to engage Margaret's lovely blue eyes, trying to assess her willingness to know all there was to tell. And she sensed danger. Springing up from her floral throne, Margaret bounded across the living room as if ready to backhand a powerful serve. She stopped at the base of a wide, arching stairway, and turned, saying, "Well, let's go upstairs and say hello to our 'boo-boo boy'! And I'll just tell him to put on his 'happy face'." With eyes wide, I followed her wondering what I would find above.

Charles was in a hospital bed in the center of a wide library with a view of the bay. His hair was freshly combed and he incongruously was wearing a satin smoking jacket straight out of a 30's movie. "Don't we look handsome this morning?" chirped Margaret, circling his bed as if he were a used car she was hyping. "But that's not very nice, the way your pillow is all rumpled, Charlie." She darted over, pushed him forward, and fluffed his pillow until it was perfect. Charlie, looked at me from the corner of his eye; he seemed in pain. But I wasn't sure from what yet. "Well, I'll just leave you two for now," said Margaret arranging the glasses and water pitcher and heading for the door. "I'll wrap your flowers so you can take them with....". And she was gone.

I thought I heard Charlie exhale.

We were both quiet for a moment, watching each other after Margaret left the room. I wondered how Charlie would present himself, with a 'happy face', or with a candid appraisal of an illness not known for subtleties. Introducing myself, I waited for him to set the direction of our conversation.

Charlie shifted positions in the bed, wincing slightly. The whole affair seemed to embarrass him. For most of his life, I learned, he had been President or CEO of one international company after another. Negotiating mergers, arranging acquisitions, and never not prevailing. Charlie and Margaret had lived in Rome for several years, then London, and finally retired to this exquisite bayside estate from his company's Sydney offices. It seemed as if their charmed life would go on forever.

"Well," Charlie said at last, turning to me with the raised eyebrows and slightly tilted head of an executive who's found a sliver of time for a vaguely annoying employee. "Let's hear what you've got?"

I explained who I was and again, why I had come. I spared nothing about the kind of treatments necessary to care for his radiation damaged legs, but I also told him it would be much less painful if he were willing to take some medicine beforehand. All the while Charlie listened quietly, gazing at his bedclothes and nodding slightly. It was if there were a medical ledger sheet he was assessing in his head. He also was clearly evaluating the pain versus gain of the proposed treatments and my ability to carry them out. I was on a job interview.

After a period of silence, Charlie turned to me and said, "Very well, I agree. But in the interest of and consideration for my wife, I will not take any medication. You may come from 9 to 10 each morning and I will be waiting for you with all supplies readied. It is my hope that after the program you've described is completed, my wife and I will be able to complete the vacation plans that I'm sure she has described to you." While I'd been hired, I perceived it was definitely on a probationary basis

The debridement would be painful—and perhaps would best have been accomplished in a hospital. However, the orders called for application of a softening cream that 'liquefied' the infected tissue and left healthy tissue alone. Each morning I was to remove the dead tissue and abrade the area to expose tiny healthy blood vessels that would eventually feed new dermal growth. It promised to be a long and painful procedure.

When I removed Charlie's dressings, I wasn't prepared for what I found. The tops of both thighs as well as both sides of his groin were profoundly affected. Though maintaining control in uncontrollable situations was always my desire for any patient, accepting Charlie's determination to forgo medication during these sessions would be hard. And before beginning, I asked him once again if he would consider something to at least dull the pain without sedating him. He looked me carefully in the eyes and said simply, "I believe we had an agreement." I now felt part of a contract I truly didn't like.

Charlie didn't make a sound. I had draped the area to give as much discretion and dignity to the somewhat barbarous procedure. Only the grip he maintained on the side rails of the bed and the trembling of Charlie's legs let me know the extent of the pain. And when I had dressed the area with clean gauze and pulled the sheets back into place, he managed a smile, as he dabbed at the perspiration along his forehead, saying, "Thank you so much for your time. I'm sure this is not easy for you, is it?" Charlie's will and gentlemanly manner must have served him well through his ascent in American industry, but that it would put it to use as a nurse punished him in the name of healing was remarkable.

Margaret showed me to the door. "I hope you'll come back," she purred. "It's so nice to see different faces from time to time." I wondered what she thought I'd been doing upstairs with Charlie. And what she would think of the man whom she'd find slumped deep in his pillows, somehow withstanding the pain.

*

As the weeks wore on, two things happened. Charlie's cancer deepened its reach into his bones. And he had begun to rely on morphine now, if only to struggle into his silk pajama tops, and to try to comb his hair. He didn't really seem to care what he looked like, but Margaret did. And for her, he would permit me to administer medicines that enabled him to play the part she needed him to play—the suave, very strong man whose arm she could proudly take.

Only once did the looking-glass shatter. Despite my requests to discontinue the procedure, at the doctor's orders I continued to remove dead tissue from Charlie's thighs and groin. With rough abrading, I clipped away old skin and opened new blood vessels to the air. It must have felt like a blow torch. Charlie began to moan and then to weep. I stopped the 'treatment', apologizing, and promising that if I had to demand it of the doctor in person, I would not subject Charlie to anymore of the theoretical remedy to his radiation burns, one that, in fact, was now irrelevant.

Then Margaret entered the room. She was smiling brightly and bustled to the end of the bed. "Where's my happy-face?" she giggled, tickling his foot. "Put-on-a-happy-face," she sang. And then, "The Westons are coming over this afternoon for a little hello, Charlie. Let me see, you don't have your pale green pajamas on, do you? Well, let me just go find them. Better get ready, they'll be here in 20 minutes." She was gone and Charlie could only stare at the door. And then he said, "Hand me my comb."

*

Charlie died later that week. I had tried to find a time when I could explain to Margaret what was happening; how Charlie's condition had rapidly declined; how their time together was now foreshortened; that they together would no longer entertain the Westons nor sail to Santorini. Instead, the cruel reality of speaking to funeral homes and making final arrangements should be done. But Margaret was always busy, preoccupied with the myriad details a member of a symphony board or art foundation must attend to. Engulfed in volunteer organizations or maintenance of her magnificent garden, she was elusive, almost hiding at times.

As I drove toward their home the evening of Charlie's death, I agonized as to how Margaret would take this shock. She seemed to have been so removed, so much in the denial of Charlie's illness, that surely this blow would fell her. Charlie had protected her from all of the ugliness and pain. He had so gallantly complied with her illusion that life would continue to be beautiful and serene. Who would protect Margaret now?

When I arrived, she was sitting on a soft settee, alone on a wide veranda. Though she didn't rise to greet me, she was smiling, and told me she was sorry I'd had to prolong my day over what had happened to Charlie. I wanted to embrace her, but the aura of perfect unapproachability still remained. I knelt near her, told her how sorry I was, and asked if I could help her make arrangements for her husband. "Oh, that's all done, dear," she said. "I made all the arrangements with the funeral home, the pastor, the cemetery, the flowers. It's all done." And she sighed quietly. I was now the one to be shocked. "You knew that Charlie was near death, Margaret?" She looked at me with a sad smile, the first one that was not cheery and immune to the travails of the world. "Of course I knew. But I had to be strong for him. It wouldn't do to think about the bad things that come in life, would it?"

Margaret then slowly got up, and touching me for the first time, took my hand and led me toward Charlie's room.

As we walked, I could feel her pace picking up. "He looks wonderful," she said. "I put on his pale green pajamas." Near his bed, she stood a moment in the darkened room, not speaking. I think she may have put her fingers tenderly against Charlie's face. Then turning on the light, and with some of the old bounce coming back, she said, "Well, it may be just my imagination, but I think he actually looks happy, don't you?"

Put on a Happy Face: Each person's way of coping with adversity is unique. Can we let our loved one and those who care about him or her use their own styles for meeting this final challenge? What is your way of coping?

_____

_____

_____

_____

_____

_____

_____

_____

_____

_____

_____

_____

_____

_____

_____

_____

READY FOR HER CLOSE-UP

The relentless pound of a sixties' disco beat spilled through the front door of Delores' house. Even before I knocked, I felt my mood lifting, a smile involuntarily forming on my lips. But when the door opened and like a waterfall, the music burst into the open, I wasn't prepared for the swirling kaleidoscope that I came to know as Roxy.

Roxy had pulled open the door, and with a little bump and grind of her serious bulk, announced, "Get ready Miss Nursey, you're gonna have some *fuuuun* at this house!" Whether given with irony or hope, this was still the most unorthodox greeting I'd ever had. And it set the stage for all that was to come.

Roxy was Delores' daughter. Not tall, no longer young, the 60-something Roxy was nevertheless a free spirit whose heart had never left the Bronx. Now, to the strains of "Show Me Some Respect", Roxy gyrated down the hall to the living room of the house she shared with her mother. Pointing me to a chair, she poured herself a drink, and with a kind of spasm of abandon, bent straight over at the waist, forced her explosion of long red curls upside down, and finally tossed them back like Medusa shaking out snakes.

I don't think I'd uttered a word—nor could I. Just watching this dervish of hair, make-up, and neon-colored clothes took my breath away.

After downing her scotch, Roxy wasted no time in getting me acquainted with the rest of her 'family'. Though the concrete block house wasn't large, she and her mother had made use of every square inch of it. Table tops, desk tops, hallways, alcoves, and entire walls were covered with photos and posters from Hollywood—mostly from the 1940s. Some of the photos had inscriptions, but others seemed to just be famous people Roxy worshipped. "So this is my family," she warbled. "And there's a picture behind every picture!" With a loud laugh, she punched me on the shoulder for emphasis. "Well, I may have been born in the Bronx, but here we're all Hollywood!" She was big and bawdy and trying very, very hard, I sensed, to never be sad.

How Roxy and her mother had gotten from the Bronx and Hollywood to this house in small town America was never explained. But Roxy wanted me to know that the three of them, mother, out-of-town sister and she herself had been "big", "very big"

"You know, what you see in the movies is all illusion, Honey. We're the ones who make the magic happen." It seems that the three women had all been make-up artists or hairdressers to stars of the old studio system. They had applied lipstick and rouge to Judy Garland and Jane Powell, to Doris Day and Joan Crawford, and hosts of other bit players. "Young Robert Redford was the most beautiful man in the world….and the nicest."

Roxy could have reminisced for hours, running her fingers through her jungle of hair as she gazed at each revered photo, but suddenly there was a strident and hacking cough from a bedroom down the hall. "Yeah, the good times don't last forever, do they, Baby?" She sighed and signaled for me to follow. At the door, she paused briefly, looked down at her bare feet, then flinging the door open, announced with a wide smile, "Here she is….MISS AMERICA!"

Delores lay swaddled in bed clothes, transparent skin merging into the comforter and sheets and above it all, two dark eyes that seemed to illuminate her corner of the room. There was one other thing—a lit cigarette dangling from between two dry lips.

Delores at that moment looked a bit like a stick figure a child might have drawn. Spare limbs, genderless body, a balding head crowned with a halo of wispy hair. It suddenly occurred to me that in the end, we all gather in this universal anonymity—all looking a bit alike as we shed the outer self-created layers of personae. From our favorite jewelry to a signature perfume, to a hair style we feel turns our square face round, these unneeded artifacts are dispensed with like yesterday's socks. A cynic would say that we then, like featureless dolls on an assembly belt, simply wobble on toward our final destinations. Except we are not toys and our personalities don't shuffle off so easily—as Delores, from her bed, was now beginning to demonstrate.

"Goddamit Roxy," she bawled at her daughter. "For Christ's sake, where's my wig!?" The smile on Roxy's face fell away and without any bounce in her step at all, she turned and went to find the missing hair.

"Blonde or brunette?" she hollered back from the bathroom. Delores threw me an exasperated look.

"How the hell do I know? Give me the one that looks best!" For a woman less than ninety pounds her lungs didn't sound as bad as her diagnosis suggested. But when I pulled out my stethoscope, she pushed it away and turned her head. Then the coughing began in earnest.

Delores had lung cancer. As she fought to bring up the frothy phlegm and pull in cool air, I saw her heart beating frantically in the spaces between her ribs. From her love affair with cigarettes, Delores' life had literally gone up in smoke. She struggled to breathe for nearly ten gasping minutes.

Then when medication had helped the bubbling coughs subside, Delores turned to her daughter standing anxiously at the foot of her bed, and commanded, "Finally! Well, put it on!!" adding, "You ought to get one for yourself to cover up *that* mop….."

We had all forgotten about the wig, but Delores hadn't. Roxy slowly brought her hand to one ample hip, stared at her mother for a moment, then marched to the bedside and firmly perched a matted brown nest atop her mother's head. It looked as if a gerbil had landed. Delores began to rail again at Roxy's departing back, but was overtaken with another spasm of coughs.

This, I learned, was their pattern. Two women, fiery, large personalities who found themselves bumping into each other's psychological spaces at every turn. Was it to be an outdated, strong mother-weak daughter relationship they lived by, or one Roxy liked better, an "I've got the reins now" status? And nobody wanted to acknowledge the third party living in the house—the cancer that was whispering in each of their ears.

The one thing that oddly united them however, was 'Beauty'. Beauty products, make-up, curling irons, skin softeners were often spread on Delores' bed where she'd tried to ready herself for my visit. And Roxy would appear in up-sweeps, side-sweeps, and eyebrows penciled in thick like Audrey Hepburn or another day, with the pin-stripe arches of Ginger Rogers. And always, each woman commenting on the style and glamour out-come of the others' efforts—usually with salty derision. These women knew Beauty and how to use even that as a weapon.

As the third month wore on, Delores' efforts at camouflaging her pallor and sunken cheeks gradually gave way to just pulling in enough air to stay alive. Mascara and liner lay unused. And even the sarcasm stopped. Roxy was at a loss. Her mother's cutting comments had often infuriated her and yet without them, she seemed to wonder who all the trouble she took with her various 'looks' was for. At least her mother had taken notice—and for years no one else had.

And then on a hot Monday morning, I got a call from Roxy. Her mother was "breathing funny". It was different than before. And she couldn't wake her up. "What the hell is she up to now," she'd wondered.

When I arrived, it was clear that Delores was actively dying. Through the night her jaw had relaxed as she drifted in and out of coma, and now she lay, mouth agape, eyes half-open, doing the hard work of dying.

Roxy seemed as much angry at her mother as she was concerned. Without lipstick or rouge, Roxy stood vacantly, wrapped in an old grey robe. "The old bat didn't even tell me what she wanted to wear…". And I guessed there were other things Roxy had wanted to hear, but that time was now making impossible to ever be told.

With another patient's emergency looming, I called for an aide to come stay with Roxy and Delores until I could return. I also told Roxy that if there were anyone who should be there when her mother died, she should call them now. Her mother would not live very much longer.

Several hours later, the message came that Delores had stopped breathing. I arrived to find Roxy looking as if she'd been crying, but now in quiet control. "My sister is driving in…she didn't make it before…but if we can keep Mother here, just as she is...just as she is...until she comes, I'd appreciate it." And so, I pronounced Delores' death, turned down the A/C and told Roxy to call me when her sister arrived.

Hours went by without a call, until again, I found myself knocking at Roxy's door. This time, unlike my very first visit, it wasn't music that seeped out of the house, but fragrance. In a cloud of perfume Roxy opened the door wearing something white I thought might be an evangelist's robe. Inside, someone else was strumming a guitar. "Come in here," whispered a smiling, conspiratorial Roxy. "You just won't believe it." And she was right.

In the darkened bedroom, Roxy's sister was also wearing white, singing and swaying at the foot of Delores' bed. The room was freezing, but ablaze with candles, tapers, votives, and chunky cylinders that made the place dance with shadows. At the center of what had become a veritable altar, was Delores—at least I guessed it was Delores, because she bore no resemblance to the woman whose death I had pronounced earlier that day.

This woman had a cascade of platinum curls that fell about her shoulders and tiny breasts. Draped in dramatic shawls, her wrists and neck wore inches of gold and rhinestones, and incredibly, a tiny tiara peeped out from atop her head. Yet, what startled me most was the transformation her daughters had accomplished on Delores herself—her face.

The rigor of an open jaw that sometimes occurs with death is not easy to close. And the pallor that follows is a white emptiness like no other. Yet, Delores lay now with vibrantly red and perfectly sealed lips, primly smiling as if having a pleasant dream. Her lashes were long and softly grazing her burnished cheeks and her brows were perfect Joan Crawford clones.

"Doesn't she look beautiful?" whispered Roxy, now close at my ear. Delores was surrounded by dozens of stuffed animals, all staring up at her like members of Sleeping Beauty's kingdom. As the sisters began to sing together to their mother, "Be-Bop A-Lula, She's My Baby", the entire room became magical and sweet. And I sang too.

Here fragrance and a certain kind of beauty had combined with old hurts that had never been articulated, and certainly not forgiven, but which now were part of a past that could be unloosened and set free with the candles' smoke. Here artifice and paint and prickly love made everything come out right.

When the time had come and Delores was gone in all her finery, I turned to Roxy and frankly asked how she and her sister had managed to make their mother so—beautiful. She smiled, and pulled the curtain aside for a moment, allowing me to see the 'machinery' backstage. "Oh, like in Hollywood, it's all in the lighting and using good products," she confided. "But I'll tell you," Roxy said, rolling her eyes, "It took two tubes of super glue to hold that mouth shut."

And such, I decided, was the power of love.

Ready for Her Close Up: Roxy's mother wasn't always easy to love. Has your loved one ever made it difficult to express the tenderness you feel? Can you do it now? How?

_____

_____

_____

_____

_____

_____

_____

_____

_____

_____

_____

_____

_____

_____

_____

_____

PIETA: A PORTRAIT OF FORGIVENESS

I could hear the moaning as I entered the house—low crooning that seemed to articulate the rise and fall of agony. It was a call from the forest or a cave—a place of loneliness and fear. Before me as I entered, I saw three women, bending low over a bed at the center of the room. It was dark, and yet they formed a living pieta as they washed the man, stroked his limbs with lotion, and called back in whispers to his pain.

Their words, which came soft as benedictions, were somehow shockingly beautiful, and their figures, melting together, painted a wrenching portrait, a hollowed icon. I watch them move with slow sweeping gestures, the tableau readjusting again and again. Was this Art? A scared ritual? Or both, bound by the heartbreaking music of this man's pain?

I bowed my head with embarrassment. Art and literature are filled with examples of the sanctity of suffering and the searing beauty of anguish. And yet, how many of us have watched day-by-day as our loved ones struggle within the constrictive embrace of chronic pain? Cleansing and resurrective? I only knew I had come to offer him comfort and peace.

I circled the women. Their warm, supple fingers were a ruddy sienna against his whiteness, seeking the lost glow of his youth. But he was beautiful—a man-boy, maybe twenty-five. As if Goya had just departed the room, this masterpiece lay at length on the bed. His hair was black and curling against the olive paleness of his face. His lips, red and parted, were dry, at times contorting—moving. And burning out of the moist palette of his face, eyes, black, fringed—hating what he endured, yet needing to endure it.

He was indeed beautiful, all of God's eye for symmetry on display. But his life had been convoluted, I learned, and in many ways, lost, until this, his return to his mother's home.

He had been daring, risk-taking, and arrested for stealing cars in his teens. Later, it was drugs, still later, robbery. A gun was used, and at twenty, he had been sent to prison. Each week, mother or sisters had visited him. For two years they needed to fly to the distant penitentiary. Later, in a day's drive, they could reach him. But each week there was someone to hug—even if from behind a glass wall. The years had passed. He had never talked about his life there. A beautiful youth, slender and straight; sometimes when they would visit he had been quiet with side-long glances of fear—sometimes, bruised. But always as they parted, he would whisper, "I'll love you forever." And the sisters and their mother would hold that murmured gift in their heart's repository, opening it when needed to sustain themselves as the months wore on.

And then a year ago a call had come—a call none of them could have imagined. "Cancer", they had said from the faraway prison. "Your son has cancer. His lungs are ruined. We'll do what we can." His mother and sisters had barely sighed. Veterans of courtrooms and detention centers; of hopes found and hopes lost; of social worker's plans and judges' edicts; of promises made and promises broken; of rehab centers and work camps; and of enduring steadfast love—they instead began the campaign to bring him home.

But the system into which this youth could not fit was loathe to deliver him up once it had claimed him. His family's efforts were to take eight months. All the while the thing grew in his chest like a mother's fetus, struggling toward its own life, feeding on his. How could the prison guards know his cries were not appeals for attention and favors? Why should they believe that the drugs for which he begged would not be sold or bartered? Why should his pain, his life, take on a value at this late date? And so, as his tumor grew, their pity ebbed. And they were glad when his mother and sisters wheeled his moans from the cell block—glad to hand the wasted life back from where it had come.

*

His eyes opened toward his mother. Perspiration perched in tiny orbs along his lips and the room beat with the rhythm of each breath. The woman held his hand and her gaze never wavered. Seeing only the little son whose hurt she could not tame, like a lioness who would nuzzle her cub to wellness, she passed his fingers again and again across her lips. "Help me Mother", he would whisper. "Mother, help me." And her hand and her will had strengthened with the resolve of the damned to bring him respite.

It was into this room that I walked. The son's head upon his mother's lap, his sisters, like Mary Magdalenes arching over his descended form, washing the sins from the flesh. His mother's eyes were black with meaning as they rose to mine, seeking power from any source. Had I been the Devil himself, she would have been his novice, his supplicant. And she repeated the tragic words, this mantra from each of their hearts, "Help him," she breathed. "Please, help him." It seemed a command from God Himself.

And so I did. With tubing and needles, and electric pumps and wires, I stopped his suffering. With nurses and monitors, I stopped his pain. What lived in his chest grew larger every day, but it was silenced for now. And from the quietness, there welled up the true man—the one his mother and sisters had longed for. The defiance of the youth was gone. The bravado of the bandit was missing—leaving only the melancholy sweetness of a man who had often cast away love—but had only now discovered it was the only thing.

His sisters would read to him—as his mother rubbed his legs, and he would stare with smiling eyes, sometimes shaking his head with the wonder of their fealty—and always the medicine pulsated his comfort.

Yet slowly, very slowly, he began to leave them—a little at first. He would still tease the girls and call his mother pet names from childhood, but evermore, he lay sleeping or lightly dreaming, or with distant eyes riveted in the shadows. The medicine was a match for the beast in his chest, but the beast would win. The medicine had stilled its call, but not its intent. And slowly, the beauty flowed out of his limbs and his lips.

The day before he died, his mother left her place beside him at the bed, as if the invisible entity had willed her away. Yet she watched, vigilant from a distance. She had had him back for a while. Their bond had been reforged, their lives forever linked. He had had the time to tell her of the sorrow he had felt for the sorrow he had brought and she had found the grace to accept it. And at last, he died—transparent as a spirit, he lay against the quilt, black curls falling over his brow.

I took away the wires and tubes and mechanical dispensaries of his peace. I stopped the nurses in their rounds. And I wrapped his mother in my arms. His sisters lay themselves down in the empty silhouette on the bed where his beautiful form had been, finding or imaging a trace of his warmth. And together we let night fall into the room, comforting and quiet.

A moon had risen in the silence. An hour had passed. No one spoke, and I thought that his mother had drifted into a long awaited sleep, when slowly she raised her head to look at me directly. In the darkness I sensed that tears were falling, but she spoke evenly, with ease and a surrender to her son's loss that was like an exhalation.

"Some people would have said my son's life was a waste...not worth a penny. But you must understand, he transformed me and with me, my daughters." She reached a hand to touch her daughter's hair in the moonlight. "When he was young, I was not a good mother...I had...men," she said, letting the words drift in the air. "I sold myself and I abandoned my daughters you could say...and yes...I beat my son."

She was still for a while and then seeming to regain some strength, she continued. "I made many mistakes. And so did he, so did he. But during those years he was away in prison, I had something good to live for. It's hard to understand. I was the bad one, but he suffered. I had sinned against my own children...only he was paying the price."

Her daughters drew near to their mother.

"I can't explain it," she said, "But when he came out of prison, I had been made whole. When he lay dying of cancer, I was being healed. With every day that I sat beside him, I could feel my shame dissolve."

Scattered bits of moonlight played across her as she turned to me. "Someone might say my son was worthless, but he gave me the priceless gift of his death...so that I might find a new life. And I hope I repaid him by loving him to the very end."

And so I left them, awed by the saintliness flowing from these three very human women. Perhaps, I thought, artists and priests have it right—there is a sacred beauty in suffering, a cleansing—and for this mother, a resurrection.

And the moon continued to rise—and also the sun.

Pieta: The mother believed her son's suffering had meaning and in it found redemption. What do you think is the meaning of suffering?

_____

_____

_____

_____

_____

_____

_____

_____

_____

_____

_____

_____

_____

_____

DAVE AND GRACE

"For as long as I can remember she's been like that." Jo, Dave's tough-tender daughter laughed with half humor. Her mother, Grace, a wire-thin, seventy-year-old with close-cropped graying hair, darted from bathroom to bedroom, a towel precariously arranged around her chest and hips. Grace had spent the last two hours in the bathroom, and now the steam of the shower billowed out. The old woman winked that she had just been pulling out a few extra gray hairs and hoped nobody minded the delay.

Her daughter winked at me too. "She's actually been in there cleaning," she said. "Trust me, not one germ has survived!"

The delay had given me a chance to get to know Jo and her father, Dave. It was Dave I had come to see. Cancer had started in his prostate and was now in the bones of his pelvis and legs. His feet, ankles, and thighs were swollen and walking was excruciating. He was bald and stooped with sagging outlines where once had been powerful muscles. When I'd asked what kind of man he was, Dave had described himself to me as "plain". His life was "plain," and he said he liked it that way. "Born in the Midwest, served in the Army, held a factory job, had two kids. What else is there to tell." He had always been hard working and hard saving, he told me. A self-effacing member of the Greatest Generation, now he had a "nice house, retirement…and cancer." He said it without self-pity.

Over the next weeks, I came to believe that Dave also had a shrewish wife who didn't seem to care if he lived or died. "I can take it," he'd said once watching his wife's angry back disappear with a broom around a corner after she'd dished up one of her frequent tongue lashings over his 'untidiness'. He'd summed up his seventy-two years in short phrases never once using the pronoun, "I", and said it wasn't worth it "putting up a fight". Dave was a humble man.

I'd gone to Jo with questions about how best to relate to her mother, but Jo just shook her head and searched the ceiling for answers as to why these two had stayed together. "Mother's compulsively clean; it's like a sickness. When we were little, my brother and I ate outside on little tables, right into the cold weather, so the crumbs wouldn't be in the house. Dad just ate before he came home. Mom?" Jo could only remember seeing her mother eat at a restaurant once or twice or a time that her mother didn't eat or cook at home—and then only things that didn't make a mess. Grace's gaunt frame proclaimed that things hadn't changed.

As I looked around the house, at the spotless, ermine-colored carpet, the sofa cushions turned on their sides so they couldn't be sat upon, the absence of photos, plants, or dust-catching bric-a-brac, the absence of shoes (since everyone was asked to remove them before entering), I realized the length and depth of Grace's obsessive-compulsive illness. Or, thought I did.

Over the next months, my conversations with Dave became friendlier though not warm or long. We always met outside. Dave wasn't really welcome inside during the day. Grace liked to keep everything in its place, and Dave literally had no place. I would find him on his hands and swollen knees pulling weeds or at the top of a ladder teetering to clean gutters. Dave only stopped when I indicated I needed to "do something medical" and then he would stiffly collapse in a yard chair.

When he spoke, he always averted his eyes, and often he only shrugged in answer to my questions. One day, after several minutes of silence, during which I'd begun to think of what I needed at the grocery, Dave turned and looked straight at me. "I guess I can never tell you what it means to me that you come here and listen to me." Dave's eyes were filled with tears and his hand trembled on the aluminum chair as, embarrassed, he quickly turned back to stare at the distance. The autumn leaves continued to silently fall, one after the other.

I could only touch his hand realizing the magnitude of this utterance and say, "It means a lot to me, too." And it did.

Whenever I came after that, Dave would be waiting for me at the spot in the yard furthest from the house and where two chairs had been placed side-by-side. Slowly, but deliberately, over the next months, he spoke of the immense loneliness he'd felt over the years. He didn't know the name of his wife's affliction, but she always found him dirty and never wanted to talk with him. He missed talking to her, he said.

By now, Dave had a special catheter that occasionally leaked and Grace had pronounced it "impossible for him to stay if he soiled the place". Now, Dave feared she would find a way to "turn him out of the house." This caused Dave, who had for years been assigned to a separate room, to get up seven and eight times a night checking for wetness that might offend his wife in the bedroom down the hall.

It had become obvious to Grace that her husband looked forward to my visits. And one day her curiosity and proprietary boundaries were piqued. As I was getting into my car, Grace approached with hands on hips, "Don't think I don't know what's going on," she said, lips tight. "I see you two huddled out there in the yard. Is this how you got your husband?" Her voice was rising. "I don't know what he's got to say to you for an hour at a time, but I'll just bet it's not about cancer!"

Suddenly, I was watching another part of Grace, a part presented in anger and hostility, but for the first time a part that was real and human and vulnerable and—strangely, likable. I almost felt she was reaching out the same kind of sad, trembling hand Dave had extended, requesting assurance and affirmation.

"I have to put up with leaking and misery and his filth all day, and you just sashay in here for an hour or two and he'll talk to you...never to me!" Grace's thoughts were tumbling together, but the emotional theme was clear. She too was lonely, sad, and bewildered. Grace had the defensive support of her obsessive-compulsiveness to hold her tiny world together. Dave was simply awash in despair with few defenses. But Dave had responded when I spoke to his despair, and so I spoke to Grace's as well.

When she stopped to take a breath, I simply said, "Grace, Dave's illness must be so awful for you, I can't even imagine how you get through the days."

She stopped as if she'd hit a wall, and her eyes grew wide. Then gruffly, she said, "It's horrible. Whatever life I used to have just flew out the window." She paused, and with a halting breath, said, "Do you know that Dave and I used to win dance contests? We partied all the time, whenever there was a disco band, we'd go and dance with all the kids!"

I tried to beat down whatever look of incredulity was drifting across my face. It was a hard stretch picturing Dave doing anything besides driving himself to perform chores, or Grace ever allowing a dance partner to touch her in a club with dirty people exhaling dirty germs. But obviously, there was a time when these two were healthy and fun, and I was glad for them to have had that.

After our meeting at the car, I always asked Grace, with Dave's permission, to join us. Sometimes she would, usually when she needed support. Sometimes she would only sit quietly while Dave talked and I listened. She'd be anxious then, repeatedly cleaning the armrests with a bleach-rag, but she was listening nevertheless and watching.

The months had brought the end of Dave's illness closer, and in the spring, about six months after we'd met, Dave was bed-bound. Jo was spending all day with her father now, renewing the close relationship of her childhood. This time Grace's jealously was toward Jo. She saw the ease of Jo's interactions with her father, but remained at a loss as to how it seemed so natural. Still, Grace was sitting up much of each night near Dave's bed. She didn't touch him at first. But in those wee hours, she had apparently begun to practice something of what she had observed Jo and I doing.

One morning, Grace met me in the driveway. She reminded me of a student who had miraculously solved a geometry problem way above her head. Her words stumbled over themselves. "You know I sit up each night with Dave, and for awhile now, we've sort of been watching each other...". She looked almost shy.

"Well, all of a sudden, about two o'clock in the morning, he just reached out his hand and took mine. I couldn't believe it. We haven't held hands in...in...I didn't know quite what to do, so I just stroked his head and held onto his hand. He never took his eyes off of me. So I just kept stroking and stroking his head until he fell asleep. He didn't want me to go, I could tell that. So I just stayed holding his hand all night."

When Jo heard her mother's report, she glanced at me in amazement. "They haven't touched each other in forty years. Mother would never allow anyone to touch her," she said.

Jo intuitively understood that something precious had occurred during that night. She pulled back her time at her father's bedside and just let the two of them, husband and wife, sit together. Grace now washed Dave's face and changed his pajamas. And she stroked his head and talked to him. Dave couldn't speak anymore, but he watched her. And Jo and I remarked that the sadness was all gone from his eyes. They were the eyes of someone drawing love from the kindness and love of another, and they rested on Grace's face. Dave died quietly, his family gathered around him.

Only a few friends had come to call, and I was one of them. But as I completed my goodbyes and turned to go, Grace came to me and said, "There's something I have to do." And with that, she carefully put her arms around me and hugged for a long, long time.

"You taught me how to do this, you know. You and Jo. I watched you both, how tender you were with Dave, how you listened to him, how you cared about me. And I came to realize that he cared about me too." She smiled a broad, open smile. "I want you to come and see me again. You'll still have to take off your shoes," she laughed, "but I'd like to make you lunch."

As I drove away, I couldn't help humming. I felt exhilarated. The growth that had occurred in Dave's last weeks had somehow wiped out forty years of unhappiness and loneliness. Any doubts I had had about some things being just "too late" were abandoned.

Sunlight was washing through the filigree of spring leaves, and a wonderful new day was forming. I found myself smiling and humming even louder. And then, in honor of Grace and Dave, a true couple at last, I burst into song. For better or worse—I sang them the song that seemed to be written just for them—

"All you need is love...da-ta-da-ta-da...All you need is love, love...All you need is love!"

Dave and Grace: Many of us find revealing our deepest feelings difficult. Are you willing to get "emotionally dirty" as Grace did for the sake of your loved one? How?

_____

_____

_____

_____

_____

_____

_____

_____

_____

_____

_____

_____

_____

_____

_____

_____

THE FIVE QUESTIONS

She was like a bear when I met her. With lips pulled back and head swinging, if there had been claws, she would have pounded them up and down and swung them in arcs—searching for her enemy—the threat in her home, the one that lived in the body of her child.

She had raged like this on the back porch with face pressed to garden rakes, and in the dark cloister of the musty garage. She had wept, bent over laundry and once, without warning, sobbed at a Walmart in front of strangers who found her behavior strange and perhaps dangerous.

And like an injured animal, a bear gone blind or a bull stuck full of pikes, she *felt* dangerous—ready to spring, ready to bite, ready to unloosen justice on the injustice that had turned her only child into a fragile paper-doll of himself, a transparent cut-out, thin as pulp.

*

The air was hot and wet, yet the fan above the boy's bed didn't turn. The breeze that played along his little limbs made him cold. The only sound was his soft breathing, muffled slightly against the pillow, and from time to time, a gentle moan, a stirring, and the toss of an arm.

How often she had stood watching this still-life of her son. Afternoons after she had fed him soup or perhaps some pieces of egg, she would drift to his door, take up her sentry position, and watch again and again as, like a movie, his short life played out before her—but in this case, it had been only the preview.

At six, Jonathon had been a whirlwind. He was like a little grasshopper, she'd sometimes thought, running here, hopping there, appearing in places you wouldn't expect. Numbers perplexed him and even bedtime stories had often ended in tears because his mind had wandered and he'd think it was morning and time to play.

If she were honest, Jonathon hadn't been the boy she'd expected. Not that she was entitled to a precocious child nor necessarily one with an intellect wide as the sky. But, it was true, she had tried to encourage him—she'd always *thought* of it as 'encouragement'. That book called, "Make Your Child a Genius", that had ended with her slapping him for wiggling out of the chair and running to hide under a table, the home-made mayonnaise and bread and the sugar restrictions she'd subjected the whole family to in order to subdue Jonathon's hyperactive streaks—well, that was encouragement in sense, wasn't it?

When he was seven, the teachers had asked for a conference. He caused disruption in the classroom, never stayed in his seat, threw crayons, talked out of turn. That was the first time she felt the she-bear well up in her. She told them it was their mistake—if they were good teachers her son would thrive. And staring them backwards and away from her cave, she had forced them into keeping Jonathon amongst the other boys and girls, one of them—and by god, not different.

That night was the first time she had truly spanked him.

*

The social worker closed Jonathon's door quietly. In the past, the boy would have switched on the television or begun singing to himself, but now there was only the silence of the room. The worker turned to look at Jonathon's mother who, with arms folded, stood leaning against a wall.

His mother never really liked these private sessions the social worker held with her son—they didn't seem to accomplish much.

"He seems much more tired than before," the social worker said.

"Well, that's only temporary," Jonathon's mother said bristling slightly. The social worker looked at her a long time. "Your son had some things on his mind he wanted to talk to you about," she said. "Some questions. But since he's so tired, I suggested he ask you one a day…."

Jonathon had turned eight a few weeks before, and sitting up in bed, as he opened his gifts, his mother had noticed the purple circles under his eyes, made all the more obvious because there were no eyelashes left to shadow them. He looked as if made of wax, a thin, pale candle whose fire had gone out. She watched him carefully pull at paper and string. She hadn't known what to buy him for his birthday this year. She had roamed amidst aisles of bikes and boards and electronic games that greeted each virtual death with a cheer. It was in the big box store that her rage had turned to tears and back once again.

But now as she slowly opened the door to Jonathon's room, entering the little den that was dark and humid, and scraped it seemed, with the sound of lungs that dug at the air for life, she felt tired too. Only wishing to slump into sleep beside his bed, Jonathon's mother instead knelt close to the little boy's face, watching the pale lids move, noticing the thin blue veins that wove across his temples, and then, as if arousing from a reverie, he opened his eyes and looked at her.

"Mama, there's something I want to ask you...but I get only one question a day..." Startled, she pulled back for a moment. His voice had long since lost the husky tone of the boisterous boy who used to call in whoops as he swung on the jungle gym or when Superman ran from room to room. This voice was all breath, and high, like a kitten's at the back of a closet.

She leaned closer, and stroked his head. "Mama," he said, finding her eyes in the dusk. "Did you want me to be born?" She blinked, and then shook her head. What kind of questions were these going to be? Had the social worker suggested them? This was not what a boy as sick as Jonathon should be thinking about. She looked at him. And suddenly, she remembered the moment she'd been aware she was pregnant. No period for three months. No husband for a year. A lost job, the back bedroom of a friend. Had she wanted a child to be born? She stroked his hot, hairless head. "Not at first," she said evenly, and noticed his breathing didn't change. He wanted to know the truth—here in his eighth year, in the week he would die.

"Mommy was having a hard time, Jonathon," she said. "I wasn't sure how I would take care of you all by myself. But as you grew inside my tummy, I didn't feel like I was alone...we were becoming a little team." She felt him nod under her hand. "And when you were finally born, I was just so happy to see who'd been rooting for us all along...and it was you...beautiful you." She could feel her tears falling and hoped they fell against the sheets.

"I knew that you wanted me, Mama," he said softly, turning onto his side. And in a moment, his breathing began to rise and fall like ripples on the sea.

The next day was a bad day. Jonathon had awakened with nausea and had begun to vomit. His mother had changed his sheets several times, and now he lay glistening beneath a veil of sweat, his tiny legs and arms spread across the bed as if he were floating. From time to time he would sit up, eyes wide, expectant, fearful, as another wave of nausea washed over him. Sometimes racked with wretches that brought nothing, other times, producing a thin flume of yellow, the boy would then fall back into something resembling a feverish sleep.

It was dark when his mother finally got up to leave her post beside his bed. She would give him a little piece of ice before she went downstairs, but as she sat beside him, he opened his eyes, and quietly said, "Mama, why did you always spank me?" Again, she stopped, her glass held in mid-air. She gazed at her son, now marveling that she could ever have struck this tiny body. And yet she remembered. Even as she ran her hand along the bones of his hip, she remembered some of the anger that had always been so close. She had wanted him to be perfect, she had to admit that. She'd given him a name that if ever he became a judge on the Supreme Court, would sound good. She had spent money she didn't have on toys to enhance his IQ. She had arranged play dates with the right children; she had even paid for lessons in art and French. And all Jonathon had wanted to do was run in circles and leap for joy. She could feel the old anger there, watch it try to rise up, but it too was tired out, wasted away, and covered with the dust of sadness.

"I spanked you, my love, when I should have spanked myself," she smiled down at him. "Little boys like you should never be paddled, because everything you did, you did because you were happy. When I wasn't happy, I think it made me angry to see other people...even my little boy...who were. Mommy was wrong to have spanked you...instead, I should have gone to play with you."

She kissed him and he looked up at her for a long time. Then he said, "It's alright, Mama. But you've got to learn how to be happy more."

Jonathon slept most of the next day. He didn't want a milk shake, and he didn't want Rocky, his favorite teddy near. His mother read silently beside him, each paragraph ending with a survey of her son's little form. And then she began to talk, rocking back and forth, eyes half closed, she offered up an incantation, an invocation, a kind of lullaby. "You will grow up to be a fine man, my little love. You will ride horses and have a bright red car when you are big. You will play baseball and swim in streams and ski down blue-green mountains faster than the wind. You may even be a judge..." here, she stopped, smiling to herself, shaking her head at how the words felt alien in her mouth. He would not be a judge, and that was alright. And then Jonathon's thin voice interrupted her.

"Mama? Were you singing to me?" he asked. She reached over, touching his shoulder, "Yes, in a way, sweetheart." "Mama," he said almost in a whisper, "I have to ask you two questions today, even though I'm only allowed one." She nodded. He cleared his throat with a little cough. "Have you ever...lied to me?" Ah, she thought, what is that? A lie to a landlord, a lie to a lover, a lie to make yourself strong and able to hop a bus to a dead-end job? Is it a lie when you tell your son he will fly down a mountain when he lies dying in his bed? The words didn't work here, a dream, a lie, a hope, a stubborn refusal to accept what strangers told you about how his life will run out like a punctured can of gas. Had she lied to him? For the most part it seemed reality was all about how well you did that very thing. From Santa to cancer, she was an expert. And now she wanted to stop.

"Yes, I suppose I have, baby-boy. Sometimes I covered the truth with little overcoats...those were the lies...so the prickly truth wouldn't hurt you."

"I'd rather know the truth, Mama," he said. "I'm a big boy now and it wouldn't hurt so much." And she pulled him up into her arms and they sat that way a long time.

"I have one more question...." said Jonathon slowly when she thought he was asleep. He turned his head around so that it was nestled in her hair. "Will you protect me, Mama?" And she felt all her breath leave and her arms go suddenly numb. This she-bear, who would fight and kill to protect her child, knew that he had asked the one question to which she most wanted to answer 'yes', and yet she closed her eyes and spoke into his ear, "No". And the room stopped breathing.

"The sickness that you have is stronger than I am, my darling boy," she went on. "The doctors have tried everything to stop it, but it is winning over your body. But I will take you right up to the door of Heaven, and I won't leave you, I promise. And if there is danger, I will be holding your hand, sweet son."

He was restless that night, moaning and turning, putting off his covers, then grasping for them again. His mother called the nurses, who came to explain that such agitation was common as the last stages were entered. The social worker came and busied herself with paper work; and a chaplain came and prayed over the little body and its little soul. And at sometime after midnight, when the well-meaning people had gone onto the front porch to talk among themselves, Jonathon's mother went to her son all alone.

His breathing had stilled now. It came and it went—sometimes not returning for long seconds—as if it were venturing into another land. And then he touched her hand and in a small voice said, "There is one more question to ask". She could sense his fingers tighten ever so slightly and she knew his eyes were searching deep into the darkness around them and he said very slowly, "Can you tell me, Mama...has all danger passed?" His last question was the sweetest. She watched the bones of his chest rise, hover, then shudder in exhalation, but his eyes were wide open and clear—the way they were on Christmas mornings. She kissed his lips and holding his hand, unfrightened and sure, she told him, as she would to a justice of the Supreme Court, "Yes, my dearest child, all danger has passed."

The Five Questions: Would these questions have been asked if the little boy had not been dying? What questions do you want to ask your loved one? What do you want him or her to ask you?

_____

_____

_____

_____

_____

_____

_____

_____

_____

_____

_____

_____

_____

_____

DEATH OF A QUEEN

The two women hold each other's hands. One of them seems to be wearing delicate gloves, with skin transparent as parchment, a dusty gossamer that would tear if touched. The other has the hands of a laborer; strong, calloused, with veins that crawl over muscles, and clean fingernails cracked from work.

Roberta's eyes flutter open and she assesses who is holding her hands. I know it won't do for just anybody to take such liberties.

Roberta is a grand dame with an iron will. The townspeople call her "The Queen", a living artifact from a time when Southern women welded power in their households that dictated everything from who would come to tea to whose hairdresser would find favor. In her head Roberta carries a dossier on the hereditary lineage of the whole town—which families are marrying up; which families will stay in their 'unfortunate' circumstances, meaning 'trash'; and which families will forever remain the power brokers even as the town dies and there is really nothing to left broker.

But in the aging Victorian on the cobble-stoned street, up the carpeted stairs with their faint aroma of mildew, in the stifling room, where Roberta lies in the burl-wood bed she'd been born in, she remains the empress of all she surveys. And now her eyes settle on Hildy.

"You were sleeping very well, Miss Roberta," says the woman cupping the old lady's hands. Hildy, is short and round with a layer of fat covering her formidable strength. She wears her hair pulled into a tight knot at the base of her neck and is never without gargantuan earrings bobbing against her face. Hildy is a good cook; an exceptional cleaner; someone who helps to tend a large truck garden in her off hours; and she is illegal. She is also the only person Roberta trusts unequivocally.

"Pull me up in the bed, dear," says Roberta, "I want to have a better look at you."

Roberta's voice is imperious, but now barely a whisper. The secret cigarettes she and other genteel ladies had puffed for decades at bridge parties and in the basements of the grand homes along North Delaware Street have caught up with most of them. And now Roberta, too, is a disintegrating wraith who sometimes when she sleeps still lifts her fingers and puckers her lips in a dream-version of a deep nicotine drag.

"Evans will be home soon, I believe….and you…you need a little make-up on…your face." Roberta needs to make little stops as she speaks to fill her lungs with a bite of air. "I always did that for Mr. Pettimore," she says, nodding in approval to her own words.

Hildy looks embarrassed, but happy. Though Hildy has never admitted it, the old woman sees her caregiver's eyes as they follow Evans about the room, and is absolutely certain that the young Mexican woman is in love with Roberta's only son.

There is only the one problem, but a multi-layered one. Hildy is an illegal Mexican immigrant with no education or position. Evans is a 50-something bachelor banker who has been raised on the same patrician mothers-milk that nurtured Roberta and those before her. It is only Roberta's faith in her own intuition that gives Hildy the slightest hope that perhaps Evans reciprocates her feelings. But what does that mean? Hildy had told me that she was raised in the church and though she is flattered that her employer thinks she would be a good match for her son—a thought that sincerely shocked her—she would never agree to become a '*concubina*', even if she loved him.

"Come here, Hildy, and bring the make-up bag..." says Roberta.

*

A few weeks later, I find Evans sitting in one of the blue wicker chairs on the wide side veranda of the big house. It is the middle of the afternoon and he ordinarily wouldn't have been home for hours. A tall, thin man with wavy salt and pepper hair, he wears sensible glasses and clothes that must have been stylish when he'd attended college thirty years before. Now he looks tired and disheveled as he nervously runs his hand back and forth through his hair.

"How is your mother today?" I ask, unaware of any change.

He looks at me as if startled by the question; as if his mother's illness were temporarily shoved lower in his stack of worries. He gazes at me, considering what to say, whether he should breach a code of privacy that is well-disciplined and strict or explain the anguish that is written across his face. Then he glances across the lawn. There on a little stone bench in a grove of polished magnolias sits Hildy.

Her hands reach around her own shoulders as she rocks back and forth, head down, in a kind corporeal lullaby. From time to time, she looks in the direction of the porch, and eventually, rises and walks toward the back entrance of the house.

"Things have become complicated," says Evans, again shoving his hair back. "Things have become complicated..." He moves away from me and sits down on the first step of the veranda, facing the little grove of trees and addressing them with a huge sigh.

"My mother is a mind-reader, you know. I don't know how she does it...but she tells me thoughts I don't even know I have. And when she does, I usually realize those *thoughts* are really feelings I just have never known how to express." Evans buries his face in his hands. "But it's complicated."

"Does it have something to do with Hildy?" I ask.

He turns around with a look of relief. "Yes...yes it does," he says, moving back to the blue chair. "I am known in this town...our family is...a very old one. And somehow, because of all that...because we've always done everything...the 'right' way...it seemed there were just some things that...Well, my father wouldn't have approved of..."

"Wouldn't have approved of what, Evans?"

He puts his face in his hands. "I think I love our maid, Hildy."

Searching my face for scandal, societal disapproval, or perhaps a suppressed laugh, the middle-aged banker is as fragile as a ten-year old boy. "Does she feel the same for you?" I ask.

"I'm not sure." He shakes his head. "My mother told me I should be honest with her. And so I told Hildy that I had a very deep feeling for her... and that I wanted her to stay here...with me...even after Mother passes. And then...she just ran to where you saw her...sitting there crying on the bench..."

"You may have to make yourself clearer, Evans," I say. "Why do you want her to stay?"

Evans stares into the trees as if trying to meld his thoughts with his feelings, accustoming himself to the pain that love can bring.

*

Over the next weeks, the oxygen that Roberta uses, the steroids that open her lungs, the pain medicine that is meant to override her discomfort all become less effective. She struggles with each breath and it is clear she is coming near the end of her struggle.

Roberta had been a religious woman who had taken comfort in the visits of her own pastor and that of the hospice chaplain. And it was he whom I called when through her momentary periods of consciousness, she'd asked for someone to pray with her.

When the chaplain arrives, Hildy is on one side of Roberta and Evans stands at the foot of her bed. Both of their faces are streaked with tears as the old woman's breathing becomes a delicate rattle.

The chaplain speaks quietly, but clearly, as he sits close to Roberta and watches her face. He tells of an eternal life that awaits on the other side, of redemption for sins, and the hope for a new life. Suddenly, at the word "hope", Roberta opens her eyes—and then she sits up!

We were all startled. But Roberta has a mission. With words barely above a whisper, and using the last of her strength, she says, "Evans, do you want to marry this girl?" Evans stares at her as if she were already a ghost. But this 'haunter' is fully in charge.

"Yes," he nods.

"Then do it now." With that Roberta sinks back onto the pillows, gasping for air through dusky blue lips and closing her eyes in the kind of exasperated relief mothers have always expressed with recalcitrant boys.

Evans looks over at Hildy who is staring, head down, into her lap, but who then lifts her gaze to Evans' face. He crosses over to her side of the bed and bends down on one knee, a slight smile touching the corners of his lips. "Hilda Gomez, will you do me the honor of becoming my wife?"

It was only after they embrace and weep and the chaplain comes to congratulate them that we turn to Roberta. But even as everyone found themselves laughing with surprised joy, Roberta had slipped from the room, her mission complete.

"Well, let's give her what she most wanted," says the chaplain. "Let's have a wedding."

Hildy helped me dress Roberta in her magenta chiffon dress, the one she'd always thought made her look like a 'tasty raspberry'. We dressed her hair and put on her lipstick and rouge the way she would have when Mr. Pettigrew came home.

Hildy put on one of her Sunday dresses and let her dark, black hair fall over one shoulder. Evans wore a suit that made him look like—a banker. And then everyone grasped hands around Roberta's bed.

"Do you take this man? Do you take this woman? Will you grow old together and care for each other, and understand when words aren't enough, and forgive when they come out wrong, and sense each other's feelings when they are only half-formed thoughts, and never be afraid to be the people you are...?"

And silently we smiled down at Roberta, a queen even in death, who with her last sovereign act had bequeathed not property nor lineage, but love— the most precious of all gifts.

Death of a Queen: Some people feel they know what is best for others. What does your loved one think is best for you? Do you agree?

_____

_____

_____

_____

_____

_____

_____

_____

_____

_____

_____

_____

_____

_____

_____

_____

THE WINNER'S CIRCLE

The long dirt road was rutted and hard-packed. From the looks of it, no dust from another vehicle had been raised in months. It was hard to imagine someone wanting to live in this remote rural forest, yet this was home to someone who valued privacy and the leafy freedom it gave him.

After a bone-jarring approach through the trees, a structure of sorts appeared. A corrugated trailer, windows duct-taped in place with bricks and wood shimming the disintegrating structure into a questionable stability. It seemed to have been hauled into this clearing about 1950 and ignored ever since. Yet the place didn't look abandoned. The yard around the rusting hulk was littered with tires and engines on concrete blocks. Several brightly painted, though jacked-up cars with huge numbers painted on their sides were lined up in back, and electrical wires ran to grinders and drills in every direction. This was a 'working yard'—a Man's Place that gave the feeling of big promise, big plans, and lots of testosterone. That is, before Doug got sick.

Doug had been a minor NASCAR driver, and later a race car mechanic for the pros, still later he'd worked for local boys who souped up their rides and raced in circles on Sunday afternoons where their chain-smoking girlfriends could admire their macho spins. For Doug, speed, cars—acceleration—was life. The low growl of an engine that would explode into the high-pitched whine of perfect combustion was like a song. The raw skill of maneuvering that car around a track, the music's soul.

Yet the man who met me at the door of the tilting trailer bore no resemblance to the powerfully built blonde driver pictured in dozens of photos tacked to the living room's walls. Doug laughed when he thought I didn't recognize him in the pictures. "You thought that was Paul Newman, didn't ya. But them is all me. About fifty pounds of muscle heavier.....but that used to be me."

There were dedicated glossies of Dale Earnhardt, of Jeff Gordon and Lee Petty, all, I learned, famous drivers Doug had raced beside or from whose engines he'd tweaked another mile or two per hour. "Don't know as how they'd know me now," he'd shrugged, glancing at people who were heroes and once friends. It wasn't clear he'd want them to.

Doug's prostate cancer had come on early—he was barely in his fifties. It had rampaged through his pelvis and thighs, finding spots now in his spine and lungs. "Where don't I got it..." he said philosophically. Doug had a special pump that was now infusing a steady level of morphine into his veins, with a small button he could push when the pain became unbearable. Now his only reliable visitor was the pain; pain that arrived early and stayed late; pain that took over every conversation; pain that left Doug bullied and alone in the musty trailer.

Yet while morphine was a weapon, he had found something nearly as powerful to force the pain into second place. Doug had created a tiny world on his kitchen table. Spread or heaped in cascading piles was a disassembled transmission, a small plastic radio, and nearby, an aging television with a NASCAR race permanently playing. For him tuning out the world that had forgotten him and the pain that wouldn't, seemed possible as long as he had a tool in his hand, a track announcer on the radio, and the television's screaming sound of cars going around a track.

The weeks had gone by. Each day weaker, Doug nevertheless dragged himself to the kitchen table to touch the metal and grease of the transmission; to touch his tools. Then one day, as I pulled into the jumble of rubber and metal that was Doug's yard, I noticed a modest blue sedan parked near the trailer. There had never been visitors or neighbors stopping by to call, no telephoned greetings from well-wishers. It wasn't in Doug's nature to talk about things he couldn't control with a wrench or a gas pedal, and it was doubtful people who had known him had been told about the contest he was waging in this tin-can in the woods.

And yet, there she was when I entered the trailer. A tall, dark-haired beauty whom it was clear Doug had never controlled.

Cheyenne was his wife—of sorts. His wife at times. His wife when his car obsession hadn't driven her away or her own wanderlust hadn't forced her out. But for now, she'd decided to be his wife again.

I never learned what had brought Cheyenne back or how she'd learned Doug was ill. But her arrival couldn't have been more perfectly timed. The pain in Doug's bones had been escalating ever upwards, he had fallen several times, and even with aides and provided meals, it was becoming clear he could no longer live alone. And like the missing part to a delicate engine, Cheyenne fell right into place.

Dirty dishes disappeared, replaced by clean ones set on a TV table with folded paper napkins and a spring flower in a clean jelly jar. Scattered clothes had found themselves hangers in a closet, while the kitchen and bath fairly sparkled from Mr. Clean. Even Doug, who had sent away aides as often as he'd let them in, seemed to accept the whirlwind that was Cheyenne. Cut his hair, trim his beard, even give Doug what I presumed was the one and only manicure he would ever have, he gave Cheyenne free rein in the trailer they had once called their home...except on the dining room table.

There, with the dismantled transmission, Doug drew the line.

"I'm a sick man! Don't you be mess'n with my car parts, woman!" he would shout weakly from the tiny bedroom when he heard the surreptitious clank of metal as Cheyenne attempted to clear the table piece by piece.

"This here's a mess full a' germs, you fool! It's gonna give you an infection!" she would holler back.

"Put down those gears or, I swear, I'm gonna be out there an' bust you one!" A hollow threat that now only brought tears to her eyes.

The shouting matches would continue, rousing Doug from his sedation, overriding his pain for a while, until, exhausted he would slump back on the bed, and Cheyenne would slam out the door, pouting with a cigarette in the Lazy-Boy in the front yard.

Over the next weeks, Doug abandoned his efforts at making his way to the dining room table. And he didn't seem to notice when Cheyenne had turned off the racing channel and instead of the television's whine of engines, only the quiet drawl of a country singer sang from the radio. Most of the time Doug slept in a kind of distant dream, rousable, but only when the pain broke through the medication's protective sleep.

Yet I was surprised when I arrived to find Cheyenne fuming in the living room as she took down all of the photos of Doug that had been pinned to the wall. Doug in a white leather driving suit; Doug with a screwdriver, smiling from beneath a race car; Doug with a group of drivers pouring champagne over one another; Doug with a prized trophy that along with the photos, she had also tossed into a box.

"That old man done throwed his life away...cars, cars, and more damned cars. No woman counted for nothin' against some pimped-up engine or a bucket a' grease!" Cheyenne paused to look at one photo where Doug was being kissed by a Miss-Something-or-Other.

"Naw...even some over-stacked chick wouldn't a made a difference. She'd never a 'got' old Doug...". And with that, she sent the photo flying.

Doug's condition changed rapidly in the next days. His temperature sent him into intense periods of restlessness and pain became even more difficult to control. A continuous-care nurse now stayed nearby round the clock.

Then without warning Cheyenne disappeared. She'd come into Doug's room during the night, asked to be alone with him for a few minutes, then gotten in the blue sedan and gone. Anger and ambivalence seemed to have been the raw material of their relationship, and maybe at last, Cheyenne had beaten her own speedy retreat.

Doug died on a Thursday. His cancer had taken him from within a deep sleep, stealthy and without interference, and thankfully, without pain. His body was taken to a funeral home and I contacted an out-of-town nephew he'd designated to help with the arrangements. Yet, the distant relative said everything was already taken care of—by "Doug's wife". He was coming to the funeral, he said—"wouldn't miss it!". Cheyenne had promised it would be a party.

And it was. The parking lot was overflowing, and the sound of arriving cars, many without mufflers, rumbled the air. Inside, mostly men ebbed and flowed toward the casket where Doug lay. In leather jackets with the names of racing teams, motor oil brands, and tire companies scrawled across their backs, they stood in groups or pounded each other in greeting, shook big, raw-boned hands, and laughed as they pointed to pictures of themselves and Doug mounted on panels alongside a line of trophies and a stand of flowers.

But nobody in that room looked finer than Doug himself. He lay, just as he would have wished, in full-length white racing leathers, leather gloves on his hands, and a shiny green crash helmet on his head. And on a ribbon laid across the flowers at his feet, were eight anonymous words in stick-on gold decals: "Stand by Your Man..." they said. "Although it Ain't Easy". It was a song that Cheyenne had been singing all along—though only Doug had heard.

The Winner's Circle: Doug's wife knew him and what he cherished in life. Do you know what your loved one cherishes? What could you do to provide it?

_____

_____

_____

_____

_____

_____

_____

_____

_____

_____

_____

_____

_____

_____

_____

THE DRESS OF THE BEAUTIFUL FISH

Naha and Anish sat red-eyed in the conference room of the Hospice House facility. Spring rain raked at the windows and inside the florescent-lit office, the proper Indian couple sat—two small, exotic bookends, rigidly straight, working to control the emotions that minutes before had had them sobbing in each other's arms.

Anish stood up. Small and dark, with a dusting of grey at his temples, his suit was wrinkled and his starched white collar collapsed after days of wear. He offered me a deferential bow of his head and apologized for his and his wife's disheveled appearance. They hadn't slept in several nights since Jyodti's change, he said.

Indeed, over the year that Jyodti had been a full-time resident of the hospice care home, the nurses told me that Naha and Anish seemed to have rarely slept. Although Anish still worked as a professor at the university, Naha, also a PhD. there, had quit her job to be as close as possible to their first—and only—child, Jyodti, a four-year old with congenital disabilities.

Every morning the nurses saw Naha arrive before breakfast, do the child's feedings herself, then position herself next to the bed. There she would read to the little girl, sing to her, position stuffed animals near, comb her hair, massage her little legs, or recite to her poems in Hindi that Naha hoped one day, having heard them, would make it easier for the child to learn her parent's native tongue.

"My wife is most upset at the moment. I am sorry. Our news has not been good."

Naha began to cry again. She rocked back and forth as tears spilled onto her sari and she pushed her streaming hair back toward its braid. "A little more time. That is all that is needed," she said. "I have seen the progress! I have seen it myself. No decisions now! Only a little more time, and you will see...everyone will see...she will come home!"

Anish's head dropped. The doctors had told them that there was no more time. Jyodti's kidneys were failing and short of dialysis to prolong the inevitable, it was time for them at last to begin to say good-bye.

But Naha needed to be heard. "Look at this," she said, shoving back her chair and coming close to me. "This is a lock of my daughter's hair." She pulled out a braided cord from a fold of her sari. I saw that it was 8 inches of thick black hair woven among saffron threads, a kind of rosary that ended in a long tassel, both beautiful and strange. "Could my child have produced this magnificent hair if she is so sick? And see this...!" Now Naha found a little clutch of photos within her purse, dog-earred and scratched from holding. They showed Naha and Anish bending over a crib; Naha holding a bundle wrapped in a pink blanket; Naha laughing as she planted a kiss on a tiny foot.

"She is a beautiful child with a future! I am sure of it." Naha held onto my arm and fixed me with huge dark eyes that though red-rimmed, were glittering with determination. "I have taught her a little song....Jyodti sings it with me...sometimes she sings it all alone. You cannot tell me that we should give up on child who can sing in *Hindi*!"

I glanced at Anish who sat staring at the floor. I didn't know how much he agreed with his wife. It probably didn't matter.

At last he stood up. "Naha. Naha, we must go home now and change our clothes. Jyodti never sees you in soiled clothing." He put a tired, protective arm around her, and slowly Naha let her eyes leave mine. Her petition was filed. Her position made clear. She would go home now and return hours later to resume her vigil—as either menacing defender or protective angel.

*

I had never met the little girl whom Naha called perfect; never seen her disability, but a nurse offered to take me to her room. Without her mother as guide, I almost felt I was stepping into a sacred space reserved for the two of them, there to attempt an override by my clinical eye of the mysterious faith that kept Naha—and perhaps Jyodti—alive.

"You've probably never seen anything like this," said the nurse as we walked down the hall. I didn't understand. A four-year old with a profound disability—I hadn't looked at the chart for an exact diagnosis—perhaps cerebral palsy, maybe hydrocephalus. I had seen such children before. And even though disabled, as Naha said, they were sadly beautiful.

"Do you know what a flounder is?" The nurse opened the door to Jyodti's room and handing me the chart, waved me inside.

I stood a few moments in the narrow entrance, letting my eyes adjust to the room's permanent twilight. Instead of a hospital bed for a four-year old child, there was only a crib placed in the center of a space surrounded by whirring machines that gave the occasional imperious click.

I was puzzled. Why had the nurse asked if I knew what a flounder was? A flounder was a fish. Flat, it lay on the sandy sea floor. Both of a flounder's eyes migrate to its top side so that with two visual sentinels staring up at predators it stood a chance of survival.

Then I realized the nurse had led me to the wrong room. The baby that lay in the crib could have weighed no more than twenty pounds. Its arms were outstretched and its little legs fell open like the frog's I had once captured for an eighth grade project. This baby was perhaps four months, not four years old.

Then I moved to the child's face. And it was true, I had never seen anything like it. The head was massive…but flat. It spread out on the bed, a massive, empty balloon, nearly two feet across, surrounded by mountains of luxurious black curls that made her look like a dark sundial. The eyes were positioned at the outer edge of her head, oddly blue, covered with thick membranes, and blindly wandering about the room. Only two deep penetrations suggested where a nose was meant to have been, and without lips or jaw, there was merely an opening into the soft mucous membrane of her larynx and the dart of a tiny tongue. This was Jyodti, the object of a love that bordered on veneration.

*

I didn't return to the Hospice House for several days, but when I did, I went straight to Jyodti's room. The nurses told me that Anish and surprisingly, Naha, had made the decision to no longer fight to keep their daughter alive. Machines would be turned off and the doctors expected she would die within the next hours.

Yet instead of the despair and bristling anger of before, there was now a kind of jittery expectation in the room—as if a loved one were being readied for a long and dreamed-of trip. And there was a new addition.

In the corner, wrapped in an orange drape, sat an old man. His hair was grey and poorly combed. He wore sandalwood beads around his neck and ran others through his fingers. Between his eyes was a large red smear. He was the *sadhu* or holy man who had come to the family. And his shadowy presence seemed to have changed everything.

Naha came to greet me at the door. "So you were able to meet Jyodti! I am so very glad that you came to see her," she told me. "Come look now....she is dressed and ready for her *jiva*'s journey." Naha had dressed her daughter in a beautiful swath of orange silk. There were golden bracelets on her tiny arms and ankles and bands of gold at her neck and in her hair. Between her wide eyes was a *tilaka's* red dot. She was a miniature goddess.

"It is hard to bid my daughter good bye in this life..." Naha told me. "Perhaps in a life before this one, her soul had done things that needed... remediation. A debt to be paid? Wrongs to be forgiven? The sadhu says my Jdoyti made herself a gift to me to add to my karma by loving one such as her? I have accepted this now," she said glancing at the old man in the corner. "I can also believe that an expiation of bad karma from her soul has been accomplished by the suffering she endured here. And now, I pray, she will have paid any debts and receive a wonderful new body when she returns. Like an old garment...a dress that is worn out...this life has served its purpose...a new and beautiful one will come soon."

Naha went to her daughter, adjusting a bracelet and smoothing the silk drapes, while Anish stood beside her with an air of peace and even, hope. The holy man began a low chant, rhythmic and comforting.

After a few moments, Naha looked up at me, a conspiratorial smile spreading across her face. Then she whispered, "My daughter is singing now. Can you hear her? It is from another world. I think she will be dancing soon..."

The Dress of the Beautiful Fish: Some things are true and some only seem true. Have you had what others might say are unwarranted hopes or beliefs about the outcome for your loved one? Are there other possibilities to those beliefs that would comfort you?

_____

_____

_____

_____

_____

_____

_____

_____

_____

_____

_____

_____

_____

_____

ROSE

There was silence in the house each time I visited. Silence of the kind that wasn't warm or pleasing or even comforting. The silence streamed from the unplayed piano, the dusty radio, the closed drapes and the musty rug. It spoke of lapsed friendships, absent family, and a deep loneliness that permeated every corner of the house.

Yet, at each visit, perched on the edge of the faded chair that had been placed with care in the middle of the room, was a tiny, very bent lady of such enormous radiance that she seemed to actually give off heat.

Rose was ninety-two-years old and must have been very beautiful as a young woman. She was still beautiful, as are certain gaunt women of personality, as if all unnecessary flesh had been burnt away by an interior fire. Whether it is the intensity of art or music, or simply the passion of living, these women only grow more ravishing as age polishes them thin and brilliant as gold.

This was Rose's case. She was frail, and her back had curved and twisted in her later years until she was nearly at right angles to her legs. She could only look up with an odd little tilt to her head, like a bird evaluating an insect. But her gaze was not relentless. Rather there was playfulness there. When Rose tilted her head atop the strained neck and gnarled back and flashed open her jet black, darkly lashed eyes, one had the feeling of being selected, of being asked for a dance, invited to a party or to share a secret. She usually smiled a wide, full smile that confirmed the thrill of her glance. And more than once I knelt down before her to peek into her face and wonder at the woman struggling quietly within this little, aging body, within this little, aging house.

Rose had cancer in her lungs and because of the curving of her spine, breathing was even more difficult. But Rose refused to discuss her illness. It was a nuisance, much like her bent frame. It did, however, perform a service. For Rose, a wondrous one. It brought people to her home, this empty shell of a house that incongruously held the vibrantly beating heart and intellect of Rose. There were memories that needed to be remembered, to be shared—and these required people. And so in some paradoxical way, Rose's illness was restorative. With each visit, she seemed a little more alive and to burn a little more brightly.

It happened then that as I sat at her feet on the threadbare rug, sometimes Rose holding my hand, and at other times her tapping me forcefully on the shoulder for meaning, that she began to recount the tales of her life.

Her youth was spent in Poland where her father was a musician who had reveled with Chopin in Paris. Later, yearning to become a painter, she studied art with an elderly master in the French countryside. It was there that she had lost her innocence to a fellow student—and then she lost the child of that romance, for whom she still grieved. As we talked, Rose sometimes wept adolescent tears as she remembered her dead child, sometimes mature tears of helplessness as she recalled the horror of World War I, in which her brother was killed.

Rose did become a painter and eventually a costume designer. She'd come to America with Anna Pavlova, the famous ballerina, whose Dying Swan costume, Rose had created. From a dusty box beneath the sofa, she asked me to pull the yellowed, watercolor sketches of opulent costumes and tattered photos of dancers and musicians, inscribed "to Rose with love" in Russian or French, recounting some hilarious night of fun.

Rose's life changed when she married an American and left her friends in the theater. She'd had a son, a husband who soon abandoned her, and finally, a job coloring photos to support her child and herself. Here Rose's tears were bitter. Yet her smile always returned, philosophical and tempered. She had raised her son, now a PhD living out of state. She had taught art, and she had published a small book of poetry—and she had survived.

The memories that flowed from Rose were, for her, a tonic that invigorated her vocabulary, animated her hands and brought her more visitors as others learned of the mind and personality of this vivacious woman. And yet time passed. At last, Rose was no longer able to climb out of bed to meet me in the living room. She slept for longer and longer periods, yet whenever she could, she would wake, smile, decline her pain medicine, and with a little laugh, ask if her visitor were comfortable because she had "a little story" the visitor "might like to hear...a little something more to tell."

Then it seemed the stories had all been told. When I arrived one morning, Rose opened her eyes, reached out her hand, white and the substance of air. Her brilliant eyes could not find me, but she held my hand tightly and pulled me close to her face. "A wonderful thing, a wonderful thing has happened," she whispered. I leaned closer. Rose's breath was strangely warm against the cool of her cheek.

"My child has come for me," she said. "She came last night without a word. She's waiting for me now; she's been waiting all these years." Rose tried to raise her head to peer into the shadows, her eyes were alight now, and it was with joy and acceptance that she seemed to know her journey with her lost child would soon begin.

Then Rose turned to me and in a voice so gentle I could barely hear, said, "I have loved you too... you have been my daughter and I have told you much." Then she closed her eyes, and her breathing drifted more and more slowly, sometimes to stillness, only to resume again more quietly.

Rose's dying took a day and a night. It was peaceful. Many friends, new friends she'd made in her last months, drawn by her life and her memories, came to see her. Her son arrived, and appeared shaken at the house filled with conversation, laughter and retold tales of his mother's exploits—the mother he really hadn't known.

Just at dawn, when most of Rose's friends had departed, and the sun was coloring the sky, I pulled open the drapes. The room was filled with golden-red light, clear and transparent as it spilled across the quiet form of Rose. It was silent in the house now, but this silence was singing with songs of life, harmonies, contrapuntal choruses of memories that had been released back into the world by Rose and into the keeping of her listeners.

The memories had nourished her, and they had healed her, and finally, no longer needing them, she had given them to others. And so, as I write this, I share Rose's treasure, and offer to you the memory of this very real human being. May you too make memories and may they be shared.

Rose: Rose's son knew her so little. What don't you know about your loved one's life, their thoughts and dreams? How can you find out?

_____

_____

_____

_____

_____

_____

_____

_____

_____

_____

_____

_____

_____

_____

I WONDER ABOUT YOU

(for my husband, Larry, 1943-2003)

We were young that year.
Our skin was bronzed and sunlight tossed your hair,
And without really wanting to—I wondered about you.

We were grown-ups when you kissed my hands
And drew me a tale of a happy life,
And you were so sure, so sure,
That though I wondered about you—
I came along and lived with you your dream.

We were seasoned when the babies came
And grew and crept and cried,
And ran and fell and squealed with joy
And made us do the same.

And cookies, baseball, Girl Scouts, crew,
Ballet, soccer, Wise Men in a play
Could never make you weary,
Never make you less than a river of love,
And my dear, believe me—I wondered about you.

And then like little ghosts, their laughter went away,
And quiet drifted down upon us,
Opaque and white and still,
Until, in the darkness of our sweet, warm bed,
I felt your safening presence and I wondered,
—maybe, it had always been about You.

Now the evening comes in shadows,
Purple, blue and thick
And swallows up my watching at the window or the wood.

You no longer walk the path with me,
Nor waken from your dream,
And my thoughts cannot protect you from the journey that you
take.

But know, my love, that gently, when color streaks the sky and robin voices
murmur against the coming night,

That I draw you ever closer, like a warm and fragrant cloak,
and watch a star's dark passing
In wonder—in wonder.

Dying is the last act of love that a spouse gives to his partner and the last gift that a parent gives to his child. For a son or a daughter, saying good-bye to a parent is the final task in the process of becoming an adult. For a spouse it is the heavy door that closes, then opens to a new life.

Yet like being born, the work of dying…for both the one who leaves and the one who stays… is not always easy. But like being born, when the process is complete, the result, we are promised, is so much better than what we could ever have imagined.

Trust in the renewal of life even as you live it and even as you give it up.

ABOUT THE AUTHOR

During her 30 year nursing career, Marina Brown worked in psychiatry at the Neuropsychiatric Institute at UCLA, and for 14 years as a Hospice and Palliative Care R.N. at the Hospice of the Florida Sun Coast in St. Petersburg, and as a Nurse Educator at Big Bend Hospice in Tallahassee, Florida—where she also taught nursing.

She has published in a variety of professional journals, including Hospital and Community Psychiatry, Perspectives in Psychiatric Care, and The Journal of Hospice and Palliative Care. She has given presentations on Movement Therapy with Suicidal Patients and The Transitional Phase at the End of Life.

Brown is author of *Airport Sketches* and the FAPA's Gold Medal Award-winning novel, *Land Without Mirrors*. She currently lives in Tallahassee, Florida.

Made in the USA
Charleston, SC
05 November 2013